TEST YOUR KNOWLEDGE OF NASCAR TRIVIA...

THE ULTIMATE CHALLENGE FOR NASCAR FANS

1. How many laps are completed at the Daytona 500?
- A. 250
- B. 150
- C. 500
- D. 200

2. How old do you have to be to race in a NASCAR-sanctioned event?
- A. 18
- B. 25
- C. 21
- D. 16

3. What is the minimum thickness of the spoiler on a NASCAR Winston Cup Series race car?
- A. .1215 inches
- B. .500 inches
- C. .200 inches
- D. .225 inches

4. What year was the inaugural season of Texas Motor Speedway?
- A. 1964
- B. 1987
- C. 1997
- D. 1972

5. Darrell Waltrip is originally from what state?
- A. Tennessee
- B. North Carolina
- C. Kentucky
- D. Georgia

Answers: 1. D   2. D   3. A   4. C   5. C

Other NASCAR books available

NASCAR 50: The Thunder of America

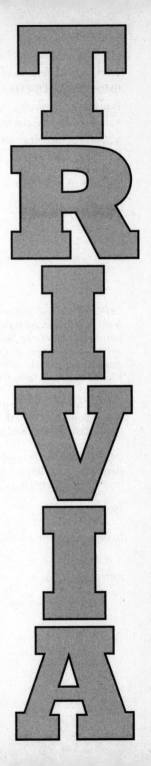

OFFICIAL
//////// NASCAR ®

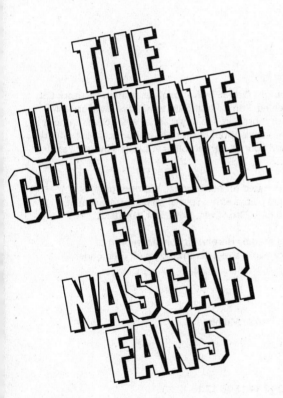

THE ULTIMATE CHALLENGE FOR NASCAR FANS

HarperHorizon

An Imprint of HarperCollinsPublishers

With special thanks to key individuals at NASCAR for their
contributions in the creation of *Official NASCAR Trivia*:
Paul Brooks, Director of Special Projects and Publishing;
Kelly Crouch, Editorial Manager; and Kevin Triplett, Director
of Operations; and including Chuck Kaylor and Lindsay Walkup

HarperCollins books may be purchased for educational, business, or sales
promotional use. For information please write: Special Markets Department,
HarperCollins Publishers Inc., 10 East 53rd Street, New York, NY 10022.

Official NASCAR Trivia was published by HarperHorizon, an imprint of
HarperCollins Publishers Inc. Horizon is a registered trademark used under
license from Forbes Inc.

FIRST EDITION

Designed by Christina Bliss with Denise Mumm

ISBN 0-06-107304-0

00 01 02 /RRD   11 12 13 14 15 16 17 18 19 20

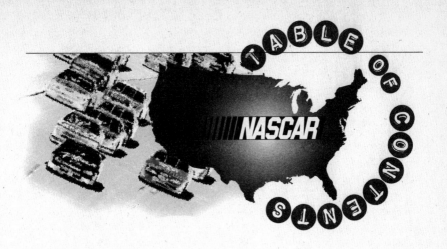

TABLE OF CONTENTS

NASCAR

INTRODUCTION

Welcome to *Official NASCAR Trivia: The Ultimate Challenge for NASCAR Fans*! We will take you around the country to each of the NASCAR Winston Cup Series race tracks, where you will be asked to answer many different kinds of questions. You'll learn details about each of the tracks as well as important historical NASCAR trivia—and maybe even a few NASCAR rules. The goal is to win the "NASCAR Championship."

We at NASCAR like to make everything exciting, so we've designed this book to be just like a NASCAR Winston Cup season. It goes like this:

- Each chapter is worth the same number of points as a NASCAR Winston Cup race (175), including two chances to pick up some bonus points.
- There are thirty-five questions in each chapter.

- Each question is worth five points, for a total of 175 points.
- Each chapter has two bonus questions.
- The bonus questions are worth an additional five points each.
- The total possible score per chapter is 185 (consider yourself a lap leader who led the most laps!).

Make sure to keep a tally of your points at each race track, remembering that your goal at the end of the season is to win the NASCAR Championship. Therefore, every point along the way is valuable.

See you in Daytona…

Chapter 1

DAYTONA INTERNATIONAL SPEEDWAY

Daytona Beach, Florida

Welcome to Daytona Beach, located on the sunny east coast of Florida. Daytona is the "birthplace of speed," and is the location of the first race of the season. You need to be consistent and earn as many points as possible to get your year started off right. Remember, your team goal this season is to win the "NASCAR Championship." Put on your gear, strap in, and start your engine—the green flag is ready to wave.

1. How long is Daytona International Speedway?
   A. 2.66 miles
   B. 2.5 miles
   C. 2.0 miles
   D. 1.5 miles

2. Who won the first Daytona 500?
   A. David Pearson
   B. Cale Yarborough
   C. Joe Weatherly
   D. Lee Petty

3. What is the maximum allowable venturi (air intake) for restrictor plates on NASCAR Winston Cup cars that race at Daytona International Speedway and Talladega Superspeedway?
   A. 1⅜ inches
   B. 1¹¹⁄₁₆ inches
   C. 1⅛ inches
   D. 2 inches

4. How many laps are completed during the Daytona 500?
   A. 250
   B. 150
   C. 500
   D. 200

5. What is the banking at Daytona International Speedway?
   A. 31 degrees
   B. 33 degrees
   C. 28 degrees
   D. 24 degrees

6. What year did the July race at Daytona International Speedway change from 250 miles to 400?
   A. 1961
   B. 1972

    C. 1963
    D. 1981

7. Before racing at Daytona International Speedway, NASCAR raced on the beach. How long was the Beach Road course?
    A. 2.5 miles
    B. 4.1 miles
    C. 3.0 miles
    D. 2.0 miles

8. Who won the first Bud Shootout (formerly known as the Busch Clash) held at Daytona International Speedway in 1979?
    A. Buddy Baker
    B. A. J. Foyt
    C. Dale Earnhardt
    D. Richard Petty

9. What octane is racing fuel?
    A. 93
    B. 110
    C. 150
    D. 100

10. What year did the Daytona 500 become the first 500-mile NASCAR race to be televised live and in its entirety?
    A. 1988
    B. 1975
    C. 1981
    D. 1979

11. What year was the first Daytona 500 run at Daytona International Speedway?
    A. 1959
    B. 1971
    C. 1960
    D. 1961

12. What year did Bill France Sr. retire as president of NASCAR?
A. 1972
B. 1971
C. 1975
D. 1969

13. What was "Fireball" Roberts's real first name?
A. Jeff
B. Matt
C. Bo
D. Glenn

14. Where was the traditional first race of the NASCAR Winston Cup season held before it became the Daytona 500?
A. New Hampshire International Raceway
B. Riverside International Raceway
C. Talladega Superspeedway
D. Atlanta Motor Speedway

15. What year did the Daytona 500 become the traditional first NASCAR Winston Cup race of the season?
A. 1951
B. 1972
C. 1964
D. 1982

16. What year did Davey Allison win the Daytona 500?
A. 1990
B. 1992
C. 1989
D. 1991

17. Who was the first woman to race in the Daytona 500?
A. Janet Guthrie
B. Lyn St. James
C. Patty Moise
D. Tammy Jo Kirk

18. Who is the only driver to win the Daytona 500 on one set of tires?
A. DeWayne "Tiny" Lund
B. Ned Jarrett
C. Richard Petty
D. "Fireball" Roberts

19. How many years did it take Dale Earnhardt to win the Daytona 500?
A. 17
B. 13
C. 3
D. 20

20. What president of the United States was present when Richard Petty won his 200th career victory?
A. Ronald Reagan
B. Jimmy Carter
C. Richard Nixon
D. Gerald Ford

21. What year did Darrell Waltrip win the Daytona 500?
A. 1988
B. 1979
C. 1989
D. 1984

22. How many years did it take Darrell Waltrip to win the Daytona 500?
A. seventeen
B. fifteen
C. seven
D. twenty-three

23. Who was the youngest driver, at age nineteen, to ever to win a stock car race at Daytona International Speedway?
A. Jimmy Foster
B. Lyndon Amick
C. Jeff Gordon
D. Bill Rexford

24. Who was the first NASCAR Winston Cup champion, in 1948?
    A. Richard Petty
    B. Dale Earnhardt
    C. Red Byron
    D. David Pearson

25. Who won the 1990 Daytona 500?
    A. Ernie Irvan
    B. Sterling Marlin
    C. Darrell Waltrip
    D. Derrike Cope

26. What was the NASCAR Winston Cup Series called prior to R. J. Reynolds's sponsorship of the series in 1971?
    A. NASCAR Cup Series
    B. NASCAR Stock Car Championship
    C. NASCAR Grand National Series
    D. NASCAR Salem Cup Series

27. What year did Richard Petty win his seventh Daytona 500?
    A. 1981
    B. 1982
    C. 1980
    D. 1984

28. Who is the only rookie crew chief to win the Daytona 500?
    A. Larry McReynolds
    B. Ray Everham
    C. Paul Andrews
    D. Todd Parrott

29. Who holds the record for starting the most NASCAR Winston Cup Series races?
    A. Richard Petty
    B. Cale Yarborough
    C. David Pearson
    D. Dale Earnhardt

30. What year did Dale Jarrett win his second Daytona 500?
    A. 1995
    B. 1994
    C. 1996
    D. 1997

31. What was the official pace car for the Daytona 500 in 1997?
    A. Mitsubishi Eclipse
    B. Ford Probe
    C. Pontiac Grand Prix
    D. Chevrolet Corvette

32. The 1998 NASCAR Winston Cup Series season was the first for what new Ford car?
    A. Thunderbird
    B. Contour
    C. Taurus
    D. Escort

33. Who is the Daytona 500 trophy named after?
    A. Richard Petty
    B. Harley J. Earl
    C. Bill France Sr.
    D. R. J. Reynolds

34. The July race (currently called the Pepsi 400) at Daytona International Speedway is traditionally run on what day of the week?
    A. Sunday
    B. Saturday
    C. Friday
    D. Wednesday

35. What does NASCAR stand for?
    A. National Auto Stock Car and Racing
    B. National Association for Stock Car Auto Racing
    C. National Agency of Standard Car Auto Racing
    D. Never Again Steal Cars at Races

BONUS QUESTIONS

36. Who has the best average finishing position at the Daytona 500 without ever having won the race (with a minimum of five starts)?
A. Dale Earnhardt
B. Ned Jarrett
C. Neil Bonnett
D. Terry Labonte

37. What university helped develop the roof flaps on NASCAR stock cars?
A. Clemson University
B. Florida State University
C. University of Southern California
D. Embry-Riddle Aeronautical University (Daytona Beach, Florida)

Congratulations, you've completed your first race. Next stop: North Carolina Speedway, better known as "Rockingham."

Daytona International Speedway ticket information:
(904) 253-7223

||||||||||NASCAR. SCORECARD

1	2	3	4	5
6	7	8	9	10
11	12	13	14	15
16	17	18	19	20
21	22	23	24	25
26	27	28	29	30
31	32	33	34	35
BONUS 36	BONUS 37			
		TOTAL		

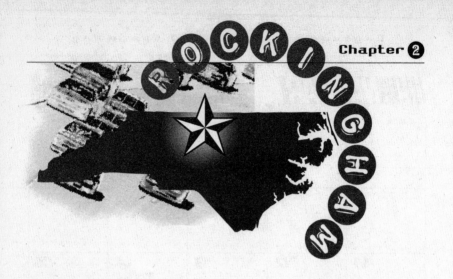

NORTH CAROLINA SPEEDWAY

Rockingham, North Carolina

You made it to North Carolina. The cool, crisp air should keep you comfortable in the car. We know Daytona probably took a lot out of you, but try to stay focused on today's event. It's early in the season, when points are critical for a successful year. Be competitive but drive smart.

1. What other name is North Carolina Speedway commonly called?

    A. The Fast One
    B. The Intimidator
    C. Too Tough to Tame
    D. The Rock

2. Who became the youngest NASCAR Winston Cup Series champion at the age of twenty-three?
   A. Jeff Gordon
   B. Bill Rexford
   C. Lee Petty
   D. Dale Earnhardt

3. How many NASCAR Winston Cup victories did "Fireball" Roberts have?
   A. four
   B. twenty
   C. twenty-eight
   D. thirty-three

4. Who was the first driver to win in four different makes of cars at North Carolina Speedway?
   A. Richard Petty
   B. Cale Yarborough
   C. Bobby Allison
   D. Bill Elliott

5. How long is North Carolina Speedway?
   A. 1.017 miles
   B. 1.54 miles
   C. 2.0 miles
   D. 2.43 miles

6. Who was the 1985 NASCAR Winston Cup Rookie of the Year?
   A. Rusty Wallace
   B. Lake Speed
   C. Kyle Petty
   D. Ken Schrader

7. The 76 World Pit Crew Challenge is annually held at what race track?
   A. Darlington Raceway
   B. Daytona International Speedway
   C. North Carolina Speedway
   D. Phoenix International Raceway

8. Two NASCAR Winston Cup Series races are held each season at North Carolina Speedway. Several drivers have swept both in a single season. Which of the following drivers is not one of them?
   A. Richard Petty
   B. Jeff Gordon
   C. Cale Yarborough
   D. Darrell Waltrip

9. What driver won the first 400-mile race in 1995 at North Carolina Speedway?
   A. Richard Petty
   B. Rusty Wallace
   C. Neil Bonnett
   D. Ward Burton

10. Which NASCAR Winston Cup driver was once given the nickname "Jaws" by a fellow competitor?
   A. Jimmy Spencer
   B. Darrell Waltrip
   C. Rusty Wallace
   D. Mark Martin

11. What NASCAR Winston Cup Series driver started the tradition of taking his victory laps backwards?
   A. Bobby Labonte
   B. Alan Kulwicki
   C. Darrell Waltrip
   D. Ricky Craven

12. Who has the most wins at Rockingham?
   A. Dale Earnhardt
   B. Jeff Gordon
   C. Richard Petty
   D. Cale Yarborough

13. The 1973 Carolina 500 had the fewest lead changes in Rockingham history. How many were there?
   A. one
   B. two

C. three
D. five

14. Who owned Dale Earnhardt's car when he won his first NASCAR championship?
A. Rick Hendrick
B. Richard Childress
C. Rod Osterlund
D. Ralph Earnhardt

15. Who holds the record for the most consecutive poles at Rockingham?
A. Kyle Petty
B. Bobby Allison
C. Neil Bonnett
D. Richard Petty

16. What is the length of the front straight at Rockingham?
A. 1100 feet
B. 1300 feet
C. 1700 feet
D. 1000 feet

17. Who is the only African-American driver to win a NASCAR Winston Cup Series event?
A. Willy T. Ribbs
B. Wendell Scott
C. Bill Cosby
D. Morris Lamb

18. What must the clearance between the engine and the ground be for a NASCAR Winston Cup car?
A. 10 inches
B. 15 inches
C. 5 inches
D. 12.5 inches

19. Who was the first president of NASCAR?
   A. Bill France Sr.
   B. Bill France Jr.
   C. Lee Petty
   D. Roger Penske

20. Until 1997, in how many consecutive seasons had Dale Earnhardt won at least one NASCAR Winston Cup race?
   A. twelve
   B. fifteen
   C. twenty-two
   D. seventeen

21. The 1989 AC Delco 500 was the first NASCAR Winston Cup victory for which driver?
   A. Mark Martin
   B. Davey Allison
   C. Kyle Petty
   D. Rusty Wallace

22. The 1992 NASCAR Winston Cup Series championship was the closest in history, with a ten-point difference. Which two drivers battled for the title?
   A. Alan Kulwicki and Bill Elliott
   B. Dale Earnhardt and Jeff Gordon
   C. Rusty Wallace and Geoff Bodine
   D. Mark Martin and Dale Jarrett

23. A NASCAR Winston Cup Series driver can still be considered a rookie if he has run no more than how many races the previous season?
   A. five
   B. seven
   C. two
   D. eight

24. How many points is the winner of a NASCAR Winston Cup Series race guaranteed?
A. 175
B. 185
C. 200
D. 180

25. Who is the only driver to retire as the reigning NASCAR Winston Cup champion?
A. Ned Jarrett
B. Buddy Baker
C. Richard Petty
D. Bobby Allison

26. Who won NASCAR's "Most Popular Driver" award in 1956?
A. Curtis Turner
B. Bill Elliott
C. Junior Johnson
D. Kyle Petty

27. What distance must a track be to be considered a superspeedway?
A. 2.0 miles or more
B. 1.0 mile or more
C. 2.5 miles or more
D. 1.5 miles or more

28. Which state holds the most NASCAR Winston Cup Series races each season?
A. North Carolina
B. California
C. New York
D. Florida

29. What year did Goodyear introduce inner liners for tires?
   A. 1989
   B. 1972
   C. 1964
   D. 1993

30. The only relatives to each win a Rookie of the Year title are?
   A. Ned and Dale Jarrett
   B. Donnie and Davey Allison
   C. Jeff and Ward Burton
   D. Lee and Kyle Petty

31. What is the name of the backstretch grandstand at Rockingham?
   A. Elliott
   B. Pearson
   C. Fireball
   D. Hamlet

32. Who is the oldest winner of a NASCAR Winston Cup Series race?
   A. Richard Petty
   B. Harry Gant
   C. A. J. Foyt
   D. Ralph Earnhardt

33. What state are both A. J. Foyt and Terry Labonte from?
   A. Texas
   B. South Carolina
   C. Wisconsin
   D. Oregon

34. What is the maximum size allowed for a NASCAR Winston Cup Series engine?
A. 358 cubic inches
B. 355 cubic inches
C. 357 cubic inches
D. 360 cubic inches

35. How are pit boxes chosen at each NASCAR Winston Cup Series event?
A. by the order in which the drivers enter the race
B. by the previous season's NASCAR Winston Cup driver point standings
C. by the starting order of the race
D. by the finishing order of the previous race

BONUS QUESTIONS

36. Who is credited with coming up with the name "NASCAR"?
A. Richard Petty
B. Bill France Sr.
C. Joe Weatherly
D. "Red" Vogt

37. How many gallons of fuel does a NASCAR Winston Cup Series car hold?
A. eleven gallons
B. forty-four gallons
C. twenty-two gallons
D. sixteen gallons

Two down—eighteen races to go. It's time to head out west. See you in Las Vegas!

North Carolina Speedway ticket information:
(910) 582-2861

//////// NASCAR® SCORECARD

1	2	3	4	5
6	7	8	9	10
11	12	13	14	15
16	17	18	19	20
21	22	23	24	25
26	27	28	29	30
31	32	33	34	35
BONUS 36	BONUS 37			
	TOTAL			

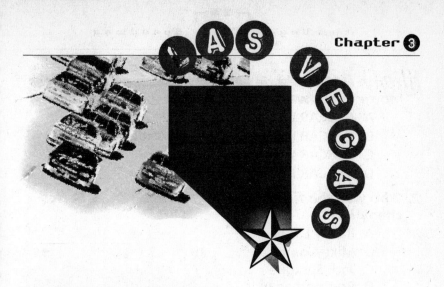

LAS VEGAS MOTOR SPEEDWAY

Las Vegas, Nevada

Welcome to Las Vegas Motor Speedway, the third stop on the NASCAR Championship tour. Las Vegas is known as a city of high stakes, which is a perfect setting for a NASCAR race. NASCAR Craftsman Truck Series knowledge will prove to be the edge here in Las Vegas.

1. **Which NASCAR series ended its season at Las Vegas Motor Speedway in 1996?**
   A. NASCAR Winston Cup Series
   B. NASCAR Busch Series, Grand National Division
   C. NASCAR Winston West Series
   D. NASCAR Featherlite Modified Tour

2. **Who was the first NASCAR Craftsman Truck Series champion?**
   A. Randy LaJoie
   B. Mike Skinner
   C. Jack Sprague
   D. Ron Hornaday Jr.

3. **What television network features the NASCAR Ride-Along Program in its advertisements?**
   A. ESPN
   B. TNN
   C. CBS
   D. CMT

4. **What car designer opened his research and development facility adjacent to Las Vegas Motor Speedway?**
   A. Carroll Shelby
   B. Jack Roush
   C. Henry Ford
   D. Roger Penske

5. **How long is Las Vegas Motor Speedway?**
   A. 2.0 miles
   B. 1.0 miles
   C. 2.5 miles
   D. 1.5 miles

6. **What name is given to tires that have only been driven for a couple of laps?**
   A. scuffs
   B. slicks

C. stickers
D. grooved

7. How many sets of tires are allowed to each NASCAR Winston Cup Series team during practice and first-round qualifying?
    A. three
    B. four
    C. no limit
    D. six

8. What was the first year a NASCAR Winston Cup Series race was held at Las Vegas Motor Speedway?
    A. 1996
    B. 1998
    C. 1994
    D. 1992

9. Where is Bill Elliott from?
    A. Hickory, North Carolina
    B. Jacksonville, Florida
    C. Atlanta, Georgia
    D. Dawsonville, Georgia

10. Las Vegas Motor Speedway opened in what year?
    A. 1996
    B. 1998
    C. 1994
    D. 1992

11. What NASCAR Winston Cup Series champion started his "Driving Experience," which offers fans the opportunity to drive a real NASCAR Winston Cup car? (It travels around the country to different race tracks, including Las Vegas Motor Speedway.)
    A. Dale Earnhardt
    B. Darrell Waltrip
    C. Richard Petty
    D. Cale Yarborough

12. What driver won the 1997 NASCAR event at Suzuka, Japan?

    A. Dale Earnhardt

    B. Mike Skinner

    C. Rusty Wallace

    D. Jeff Gordon

13. What driver is known as Mr. Excitement?

    A. Rusty Wallace

    B. Geoff Bodine

    C. Terry Labonte

    D. Jimmy Spencer

14. Who has won the most NASCAR Winston Cup races in one season (twenty-seven)?

    A. David Pearson

    B. Dale Jarrett

    C. Dale Earnhardt

    D. Richard Petty

15. Who won the inaugural NASCAR Craftsman Truck Series race at Las Vegas Motor Speedway?

    A. Jack Sprague

    B. Joe Ruttman

    C. Robby Gordon

    D. Ron Hornaday, Jr.

16. Who is the oldest driver to win a NASCAR Winston Cup Series championship?

    A. Bobby Allison

    B. Cale Yarborough

    C. A. J. Foyt

    D. Neil Bonnett

17. How old was he?

    A. 52 years

    B. 47 years and 6 months

    C. 45 years and 351 days

    D. 40 years

18. Who is known as "Front Row Joe?"
   A. Joe Weatherly
   B. Joe Jackson
   C. Joe Nemechek
   D. Joe Collins

19. Who won the last NASCAR Winston Cup race for the Chrysler Corporation (1977)?
   A. Tim Flock
   B. Neil Bonnett
   C. Ernie Irvan
   D. Bobby Labonte

20. What year did Bobby Isaac set the record for most poles in one season?
   A. 1993
   B. 1975
   C. 1969
   D. 1981

21. How many poles did Bobby Isaac win that season?
   A. ten
   B. twenty
   C. fifteen
   D. thirty

22. In what year was the Thunderbird introduced to NASCAR Winston Cup racing?
   A. 1948
   B. 1959
   C. 1976
   D. 1982

23. In 1982, Dale Earnhardt's only victory came in what make of car?
   A. Chevrolet
   B. Buick
   C. Ford
   D. Pontiac

24. Las Vegas Motor Speedway is located in what state?
A. Arizona
B. California
C. Nevada
D. Iowa

25. What year did Richard Petty win his first NASCAR Winston Cup Series race as an owner after retiring as a driver?
A. 1995
B. 1993
C. 1996
D. 1997

26. Who was the driver for Richard Petty in that race?
A. Kyle Petty
B. Bobby Labonte
C. Hut Stricklin
D. Bobby Hamilton

27. What year did Dale Earnhardt win his sixth NASCAR Winston Cup Series championship?
A. 1992
B. 1993
C. 1991
D. 1994

28. How many times has Darrell Waltrip won a NASCAR Winston Cup Series championship?
A. three
B. six
C. four
D. one

29. What year did Darrell Waltrip win his first championship?
A. 1981
B. 1980

C. 1972

D. 1977

30. What driver won the NASCAR Busch Series race at Las Vegas Motor Speedway in 1997?
A. Mark Martin
B. Elliott Sadler
C. Mike McLaughlin
D. Jeff Green

31. Who is the only driver to win three consecutive NASCAR Winston Cup Series championships?
A. Richard Petty
B. Dale Earnhardt
C. Lee Petty
D. Cale Yarborough

32. When was the last NASCAR Winston Cup dirt track race run (in Raleigh, North Carolina)?
A. 1963
B. 1970
C. 1985
D. 1994

33. Las Vegas Motor Speedway is new to NASCAR racing. What is the oldest NASCAR-sanctioned race track?
A. Bowman Gray Stadium (Winston-Salem, North Carolina)
B. Martinsville Speedway
C. Daytona International Speedway
D. Charlotte Motor Speedway

34. What does the blue flag with an orange stripe signify?
A. enter the pits
B. start/restart of the race
C. slower/lapped traffic must move over
D. one lap to go

35. **Four tire companies have produced tires for NASCAR racing. Which of the following companies has never been a tire supplier of NASCAR?**
   A. Dunlop
   B. Goodyear
   C. Hoosier
   D. Firestone

BONUS QUESTIONS

36. **What driver holds the NASCAR Winston Cup Series record for most NASCAR Winston Cup wins?**
   A. Richard Petty
   B. Bill Elliott
   C. Jeff Gordon
   D. Rusty Wallace

37. **How many NASCAR Winston Cup races did Richard Petty win?**
   A. 45
   B. 360
   C. 2,152
   D. 200

You made it through another race. Did you take a gamble and go for the win or did you sit tight and play it conservatively? Points will win you a championship. See you at Darlington . . .

Las Vegas Motor Speedway ticket information:
   (702) 644-4443

║║║║NASCAR® SCORECARD

1	2	3	4	5
6	7	8	9	10
11	12	13	14	15
16	17	18	19	20
21	22	23	24	25
26	27	28	29	30
31	32	33	34	35
BONUS 36	BONUS 37			
		TOTAL		

Answer Key for Chapter Three

1. C   2. B   3. A   4. A   5. D   6. A   7. A   8. B   9. D
10. A   11. C   12. B   13. D   14. D   15. A   16. A   17. C   18. C
19. B   20. C   21. B   22. B   23. C   24. C   25. C   26. D   27. B
28. A   29. A   30. D   31. D   32. B   33. A   34. C   35. A   36. A
37. D

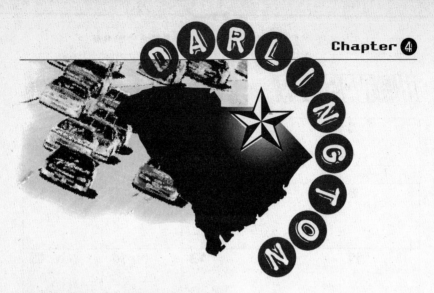

DARLINGTON RACEWAY

Darlington, South Carolina

Here we are in Darlington, South Carolina. This track has been called many things, but the one every driver should remember is the track that's "Too Tough to Tame." Race hard but smart, and don't forget to take it easy in Turn Four.

1. Who are the only two drivers to ever win the Winston Million?
   A. Jeff Gordon and Michael Waltrip
   B. Bill Elliott and Dale Earnhardt
   C. Bill Elliott and Jeff Gordon
   D. Dale Jarrett and Sterling Marlin

2. What years did they win it, respectively?
    A. 1985 and 1997
    B. 1980 and 1995
    C. 1987 and 1997
    D. 1990 and 1996

3. What year was NASCAR founded?
    A. 1947
    B. 1942
    C. 1950
    D. 1933

4. What year did NASCAR sanction its first race?
    A. 1947
    B. 1948
    C. 1953
    D. 1967

5. What is the minimum weight required, not counting the driver, for a NASCAR Winston Cup Series car in 1998?
    A. 3400 pounds
    B. 3500 pounds
    C. 3700 pounds
    D. 3000 pounds

6. Who was the first driver to win the Southern 500 at Darlington three times?
    A. Herb Thomas
    B. Jeff Gordon
    C. Buddy Baker
    D. Morgan Shepherd

7. How old do you have to be to race in a NASCAR-sanctioned event?
    A. eighteen
    B. twenty-five
    C. twenty-one
    D. sixteen

8. Who was the first driver to win three consecutive Southern 500 races at Darlington?
   A. Herb Thomas
   B. Jeff Gordon
   C. Buddy Baker
   D. Morgan Shepard

9. What Indy driver won the first Southern 500?
   A. A. J. Foyt
   B. Johnny Mantz
   C. Mario Andretti
   D. Al Unser Jr.

10. How many crew members are allowed "over the wall" during a NASCAR Winston Cup Series pit stop?
   A. five
   B. eleven
   C. seven
   D. as many as the team wants

11. What year was Alan Kulwicki's rookie season in the NASCAR Winston Cup Series?
   A. 1985
   B. 1986
   C. 1980
   D. 1982

12. What year was the first Southern 500 at Darlington Raceway held?
   A. 1954
   B. 1961
   C. 1950
   D. 1960

13. How many cars started the first NASCAR Grand National Series (currently known as the NASCAR Winston Cup Series) race at Darlington?
   A. forty-three
   B. forty-two

C. seventy-five
D. twenty-four

14. What three parts of a NASCAR Winston Cup car must be stock?
A. headlights, front bumper, and driver's seat
B. roof, spoiler, and rear quarter panels
C. hood, roof, and tires
D. hood, roof, and deck lid

15. Ned Jarrett holds the NASCAR Winston Cup record for greatest margin of victory in one race. He won the 1965 Southern 500 by how many laps?
A. two
B. eleven
C. fourteen
D. twenty-three

16. What is the distance of Darlington Raceway?
A. 1 mile
B. 1.366 miles
C. 1.732 miles
D. 2.4 miles

17. Who holds Darlington Raceway's track speed record at 139.958 mph?
A. Jeff Gordon
B. Ernie Irvan
C. David Pearson
D. Dale Earnhardt

18. What was the last year Dodge won a NASCAR-sanctioned race?
A. never won a race
B. 1970
C. 1977
D. 1980

19. What former NFL football coach currently owns a NASCAR Winston Cup Series team?
    A. Joe Gibbs
    B. Tom Landry
    C. John Madden
    D. Don Shula

20. As of 1998, which team does Joe Gibbs own?
    A. #3 GM Goodwrench Chevrolet
    B. #18 Interstate Batteries Pontiac
    C. #30 Pennzoil Pontiac
    D. #10 Tide Ford

21. Which driver has won the most NASCAR-sanctioned races (10) at Darlington Raceway?
    A. Richard Petty
    B. David Pearson
    C. Dale Earnhardt
    D. Darrell Waltrip

22. What was the first year Goodyear tires were used in NASCAR Winston Cup racing?
    A. 1959
    B. 1963
    C. 1957
    D. 1970

23. What year was the last Southern 500 held on Labor Day (a Monday)?
    A. 1990
    B. 1984
    C. 1975
    D. 1980

24. How many women have competed in NASCAR Winston Cup competition?
    A. ten
    B. six
    C. three
    D. none

25. **The Winston Million was offered from 1985 through 1997 and was won twice. To win it a driver must win three of the four "Crown Jewel" NASCAR Winston Cup Series races in one season. Which were they?**
   A. Daytona 500, Busch Clash, Winston 500, and Brickyard 400
   B. Brickyard 400, Coca-Cola 600, Winston 500, and Mountain Dew Southern 500
   C. Daytona 500, Brickyard 400, Winston 500, and Coca-Cola 600
   D. Daytona 500, Winston 500, Coca-Cola 600, and Mountain Dew Southern 500

26. **Who holds the record for sitting on the pole the most times (twelve) at Darlington Raceway?**
   A. David Pearson
   B. Richard Petty
   C. Joe Nemechek
   D. Jeff Gordon

27. **What year was Darlington Raceway "flipped," so that the new start/finish line was on the old backstretch?**
   A. 1996
   B. 1997
   C. 1998
   D. 1990

28. **Which driver holds the record for most consecutive starts (569) in NASCAR Winston Cup Series history (through the 1997 season)?**
   A. Richard Petty
   B. Terry Labonte
   C. Junior Johnson
   D. Bill Elliott

29. At the Mountain Dew Southern 500, in 1996, Dale Jarrett raced for the Winston Million and Hut Stricklin led the most laps, but who won the race?
A. Bill Elliott
B. Bobby Labonte
C. Sterling Marlin
D. Jeff Gordon

30. Who was the 1997 NASCAR Winston Cup Champion?
A. Dale Earnhardt
B. Mark Martin
C. Dale Jarrett
D. Jeff Gordon

31. What make of car won the first NASCAR Winston Cup race?
A. Monte Carlo
B. Lincoln
C. Hudson Hornet
D. Thunderbird

32. Who was the 1997 NASCAR Busch Series champion?
A. Steve Park
B. Randy LaJoie
C. Mark Martin
D. Todd Bodine

33. Who won the 1989 NASCAR Winston Cup Rookie of the Year title?
A. Jeff Gordon
B. Davey Allison
C. Dick Trickle
D. Kyle Petty

34. How many drivers have won back-to-back NASCAR Winston Cup championships?
A. two
B. seven
C. ten
D. fourteen

35. What driver holds the all-time NASCAR Winston Cup Series record for most poles in one season?
A. Bobby Isaac
B. Richard Petty
C. Dale Earnhardt
D. Jimmy Spencer

BONUS QUESTIONS

36. Who was the first winner of the Winston Select?
A. Darrell Waltrip
B. Richard Petty
C. Bobby Allison
D. Bill Elliott

37. What was the first year NASCAR Winston Cup Series teams raced in Japan?
A. 1995
B. 1997
C. 1984
D. 1996

No time for breaks. We're headed to Bristol for a little short-track racin'.

Darlington Raceway ticket information:
(803) 395-8499

//////NASCAR. SCORECARD

1	2	3	4	5
6	7	8	9	10
11	12	13	14	15
16	17	18	19	20
21	22	23	24	25
26	27	28	29	30
31	32	33	34	35
BONUS 36	BONUS 37			
	TOTAL			

Chapter 5

BRISTOL MOTOR SPEEDWAY

Bristol, Tennessee

Welcome to Bristol! This place can be fun, but it's easy to get caught up in someone else's problems. Let's not forget about points—even if we're a little behind, we have plenty of time to make them up. Bristol has never been easy for any driver, so give it your best shot.

1. What track is known as the world's fastest half-mile?
    A. Martinsville Speedway
    B. Bristol Motor Speedway
    C. North Wilkesboro Speedway
    D. New Hampshire International Speedway

2. What driver has won seven NASCAR Winston Cup Series races in a row at Bristol Motor Speedway?
>   A. Kyle Petty
>   B. Dale Earnhardt
>   C. Darrell Waltrip
>   D. Donnie Allison

3. Bill Rexford is the youngest NASCAR Winston Cup Series champion (1950) ever crowned. How old was he?
>   A. 18 years 20 days
>   B. 23 years 229 days
>   C. 16 years 380 days
>   D. 30 years 2 days

4. If qualifying for a NASCAR Winston Cup Series race is rained out, how is the starting order determined?
>   A. By last name
>   B. By car owner points
>   C. By current driver point standings
>   D. By the finishing order of the previous race

5. If a driver change is made during a race after the first full lap is completed, who receives the points?
>   A. The driver who started the race
>   B. The driver who finishes the race
>   C. The driver who races the most laps
>   D. The car owner decides

6. What type of surface does Bristol Motor Speedway have?
>   A. concrete
>   B. dirt
>   C. asphalt
>   D. clay

7. What company owns Bristol Motor Speedway?
>   A. International Speedway Corporation
>   B. Penske Speedway Holding Corporation
>   C. Speedway Motorsports, Inc.
>   D. Kaisers Ventures, Inc.

8. What is the penalty for running over an air hose during a pit stop?
   A. disqualification from the race
   B. a stop and go penalty
   C. a ten-second penalty
   D. a one-lap penalty

9. How many bonus points does a NASCAR Winston Cup Series driver get for leading the most laps?
   A. ten
   B. eight
   C. five
   D. fifteen

10. What is the minimum thickness of the spoiler on a NASCAR Winston Cup Series race car?
   A. .125 inches
   B. .500 inches
   C. .200 inches
   D. .225 inches

11. What did the land on which Bristol Motor Speedway was built used to be?
   A. a graveyard
   B. a football stadium
   C. a dairy farm
   D. a goat farm

12. Who is the only driver to start from the pole, lead every lap, and win at Bristol in a single NASCAR Winston Cup Series race?
   A. Cale Yarborough
   B. Rusty Wallace
   C. Sterling Marlin
   D. Kenny Wallace

13. What drivers combined to win the first NASCAR Winston Cup race at Bristol (1961)?
 A. Junior Johnson and Darrell Waltrip
 B. David Pearson and Dale Earnhardt
 C. Jack Smith and Johnny Allen
 D. Lee Petty and Buck Baker

14. Which former NASCAR Winston Cup Series champion won his first NASCAR Winston Cup Series race at Bristol Motor Speedway?
 A. David Pearson
 B. Alan Kulwicki
 C. Rusty Wallace
 D. Jeff Gordon

15. Bristol Motor Speedway could have very easily been opened in 1961 under what name?
 A. Tennessee Motor Speedway
 B. Volunteer Raceway
 C. Piney Flats International Speedway
 D. Tennessee Raceway

16. Who won the last NASCAR Winston Cup Series race at North Wilkesboro Speedway?
 A. Brett Bodine
 B. Jeff Gordon
 C. Terry Labonte
 D. Mike Wallace

17. Forty-two cars started the first race at Bristol Motor Speedway. How many finished?
 A. thirty
 B. nineteen
 C. twenty-eight
 D. forty-one

18. Originally, the banking at Bristol was twenty-two degrees. What is it now?
 A. forty degrees
 B. twenty-eight degrees

C. forty-two degrees
D. thirty-six degrees

19. What year was the first night NASCAR Winston Cup Series race held at Bristol Motor Speedway?
A. 1978
B. 1985
C. 1971
D. 1990

20. Who was the 1979 NASCAR Winston Cup Series Rookie of the Year?
A. Geoff Bodine
B. Dale Earnhardt
C. Bill Elliott
D. Bobby Labonte

21. What is Rick Hendrick's first name?
A. Joseph
B. Charles
C. Robert
D. Richard

22. Who has the most NASCAR Winston Cup Series wins at Bristol?
A. Dale Jarrett
B. Darrell Waltrip
C. Cale Yarborough
D. David Pearson

23. Only one driver has driven a Buick into victory lane at Bristol (three times). Who was it?
A. Terry Labonte
B. David Pearson
C. Darrell Waltrip
D. Cale Yarborough

24. Who was the first driver to win back-to-back NASCAR Winston Cup championships?
A. Darrell Waltrip
B. Cale Yarborough
C. Richard Petty
D. Buck Baker

25. Who is the only driver to win NASCAR's Winston Cup Rookie of the Year one year and the NASCAR Winston Cup championship the next?
A. Davey Allison
B. Bill Elliott
C. Jeff Gordon
D. Dale Earnhardt

26. What was originally in the infield at Bristol Motor Speedway?
A. a used car lot
B. a football field
C. a circus
D. a baseball diamond

27. What year did Robert Yates become the sole owner of his NASCAR Winston Cup Series team?
A. 1988
B. 1990
C. 1986
D. 1987

28. Who was the first driver to win three NASCAR Winston Cup championships?
A. Cale Yarborough
B. A. J. Foyt
C. Richard Petty
D. Lee Petty

29. Bristol Motor Speedway was a perfect half-mile when it opened. How long is it now?
A. .600 mile
B. .488 mile

C. .533 mile
D. .650 mile

30. Harry Gant is the oldest winner of a NASCAR Winston Cup championship. What year did he win it?
   A. 1964
   B. 1992
   C. 1984
   D. 1975

31. What team did Ricky Rudd leave to start his own NASCAR Winston Cup Series team?
   A. Robert Yates Racing
   B. Roush Racing
   C. Penske Racing South
   D. Hendrick Motorsports

32. How many NASCAR Winston Cup races were won by the Allison brothers?
   A. 7
   B. 23
   C. 94
   D. 102

33. Where was the last NASCAR Winston Cup race held on a dirt track?
   A. Raleigh, North Carolina
   B. Darlington, South Carolina
   C. Martinsville, Virginia
   D. Loudon, New Hampshire

34. What was the first year Winston became the sponsor of the NASCAR Winston Cup Series?
   A. 1971
   B. 1948
   C. 1956
   D. 1969

35. Which foreign car has won a NASCAR race?
A. Jaguar
B. Porsche
C. Ferrari
D. Lamborghini

BONUS QUESTIONS

36. Who holds the record for the most career NASCAR Winston Cup wins from the pole position?
A. Dale Earnhardt
B. David Pearson
C. Richard Petty
D. Ned Jarrett

37. How many victories from the pole does the above record holder have?
A. sixty-one
B. fifty-nine
C. thirty-two
D. forty-four

Great job! Next track: Texas Motor Speedway.

Bristol Motor Speedway ticket information:
(423) 764-1161

//////NASCAR. SCORECARD

1	2	3	4	5
6	7	8	9	10
11	12	13	14	15
16	17	18	19	20
21	22	23	24	25
26	27	28	29	30
31	32	33	34	35
BONUS 36	BONUS 37			
		TOTAL		

Chapter 6

TEXAS MOTOR SPEEDWAY

Fort Worth, Texas

Welcome to the Lone Star State and Texas Motor Speedway. This is a newer track, but the competition is still tough in the sixth race of the season, so keep a close watch on your points, take your time, and concentrate.

1. **Who won the inaugural NASCAR Winston Cup race at Texas Motor Speedway?**
   A. Jeff Burton
   B. Mark Martin
   C. Dale Jarrett
   D. Bobby Labonte

2. **Who is known as "the fastest man in NASCAR"?**
   A. Dale Earnhardt
   B. Jeff Gordon
   C. Bill Elliott
   D. John Andretti

3. **What driver holds the all-time NASCAR Winston Cup Series record for the most consecutive years (twenty) in which he won at least one pole?**
   A. Ned Jarrett
   B. Richard Petty
   C. Mark Martin
   D. David Pearson

4. **What year was the inaugural season of Texas Motor Speedway?**
   A. 1964
   B. 1987
   C. 1997
   D. 1972

5. **What is the longest amount of time between a driver's first NASCAR Winston Cup championship and his second?**
   A. twenty-five years
   B. ten years
   C. seventeen years
   D. twelve years

6. Who went the longest between those championships?
   A. Terry Labonte
   B. Jeff Gordon
   C. Ted Musgrave
   D. Richard Petty

7. Who was the first NASCAR Winston Cup Series driver to test tires at Texas Motor Speedway?
   A. Hut Stricklin
   B. Rusty Wallace
   C. Mark Martin
   D. Ted Musgrave

8. What year did Richard Petty win his first NASCAR Winston Cup championship?
   A. 1970
   B. 1964
   C. 1960
   D. 1967

9. What year did Richard Petty win the last of his seven NASCAR Winston Cup championships?
   A. 1984
   B. 1980
   C. 1979
   D. 1978

10. How long is Texas Motor Speedway?
   A. 1.0 miles
   B. 1.5 miles
   C. 2.0 miles
   D. 1.8 miles

11. What driver won the first NASCAR Winston Cup Series race held in Japan (1996)?
   A. Rusty Wallace
   B. Dale Earnhardt
   C. Mike Skinner
   D. Ricky Craven

12. What year was the fuel cell introduced?
   A. 1949
   B. 1956
   C. 1965
   D. 1986

13. What year did Terry Labonte compete in his first NASCAR Winston Cup Series race?
   A. 1977
   B. 1978
   C. 1980
   D. 1994

14. At which track did Terry Labonte run his first race?
   A. Martinsville Speedway
   B. Watkins Glen International
   C. Darlington Raceway
   D. Talladega Superspeedway

15. Who was the pole sitter for the inaugural NASCAR Winston Cup Series race at Texas in 1997?
   A. Morgan Shepherd
   B. Joe Nemecheck
   C. Jeff Burton
   D. Dale Jarrett

16. How many NASCAR Winston Cup races did Jeff Gordon win in his 1995 NASCAR Winston Cup championship season?
   A. eight
   B. ten
   C. six
   D. seven

17. Which of the following NASCAR Winston Cup drivers is from Texas?
   A. Bobby Hillin
   B. Rick Mast
   C. Darrell Waltrip
   D. Bobby Hamilton

18. What is the minimum size a NASCAR Winston Cup Series engine can be?
 A. 351 cubic inches
 B. 352 cubic inches
 C. 350 cubic inches
 D. 349 cubic inches

19. What driver ran the fastest qualifying lap at Texas in 1997?
 A. Joe Nemechek
 B. Jeff Burton
 C. No one, it was not held due to inclement weather
 D. Rusty Wallace

20. Who was the first NASCAR Winston Cup driver to win more than $500,000 in a single season (1978)?
 A. Cale Yarborough
 B. Dale Earnhardt
 C. Darrell Waltrip
 D. Richard Petty

21. What driver won the first NASCAR Busch Series race at Texas Motor Speedway?
 A. Mark Martin
 B. Steve Park
 C. Randy LaJoie
 D. Mike McLaughlin

22. Who was the first NASCAR Winston Cup driver to use a radio to communicate with his crew?
 A. Richard Petty
 B. Jack Smith
 C. LeeRoy Yarborough
 D. Jeff Gordon

23. What driver won the inaugural NASCAR Craftsman Truck Series race at Texas Motor Speedway?
 A. Mike Skinner
 B. Kenny Irwin Jr

C. Ron Hornaday Jr.
D. Jack Sprague

24. How did "Fireball" Roberts get his nickname?
   A. He had bright red hair.
   B. He started racing at Firebird Speedway.
   C. He had a hot temper.
   D. Because of the fastball he threw during his high school baseball games.

25. The turns at Texas Motor Speedway have banking of eight and ___ degrees.
   A. thirty-one
   B. twelve
   C. twenty-four
   D. eighteen

26. Who was the 1976 NASCAR Winston Cup Series champion?
   A. Cale Yarborough
   B. Jack Ingram
   C. Darrell Waltrip
   D. J. D. McDuffie

27. How many wins did the 1976 NASCAR Winston Cup Series champion have that season?
   A. five
   B. four
   C. eleven
   D. nine

28. What year did Bill France Jr. become president of NASCAR?
   A. 1972
   B. 1975
   C. 1980
   D. 1987

29. How many NASCAR Winston Cup races did Junior Johnson win as a car owner?
   A. 20
   B. 140
   C. 79
   D. 123

30. What year did Bill Elliott win his first NASCAR Winston Cup race?
   A. 1981
   B. 1988
   C. 1979
   D. 1983

31. At which track did Bill Elliott win his first NASCAR Winston Cup race?
   A. Daytona International Speedway
   B. Riverside International Raceway
   C. North Carolina Speedway
   D. Charlotte Motor Speedway

32. What is the record number of lead changes for a NASCAR Winston Cup race (Talladega, 1984)?
   A. four
   B. fifty-six
   C. seventy-five
   D. ninety-eight

33. Construction began on Texas Motor Speedway in what year?
   A. 1956
   B. 1971
   C. 1989
   D. 1995

34. What year did Richard Petty win his fifth NASCAR Winston Cup Championship?
   A. 1974
   B. 1972

C. 1976
D. 1970

35. Which driver won the first NASCAR Winston Cup race for car owner Richard Childress (1983)?
A. Ricky Rudd
B. Dale Earnhardt
C. Mike Skinner
D. Alan Kulwicki

BONUS QUESTIONS

36. Who was the 1984 NASCAR Winston Cup Series champion?
A. Darrell Waltrip
B. Bobby Allison
C. Terry Labonte
D. Lake Speed

37. How many points did he win by?
A. seventy
B. ten
C. sixty-five
D. twenty-five

Martinsville is waiting. It's one of NASCAR's oldest tracks and is full of tradition. See you next weekend . . .

Texas Motor Speedway ticket information:
(817) 215-8500

NASCAR. SCORECARD

1	2	3	4	5
6	7	8	9	10
11	12	13	14	15
16	17	18	19	20
21	22	23	24	25
26	27	28	29	30
31	32	33	34	35
BONUS 36	BONUS 37			
		TOTAL		

Chapter 7

MARTINSVILLE SPEEDWAY

Martinsville, Virginia

Here we are in Martinsville, Virginia. If you conserve your brakes and tires you should have no problem finishing the race with plenty of points. Of course, finishing well at Martinsville is easier said than done...

1. Who became the first NASCAR Winston Cup race sponsor for Martinsville Speedway?
   A. Air National Guard
   B. Ford
   C. Pepsi
   D. Virginia National Bank

2. **What year did Ernie Irvan win his first NASCAR Winston Cup Series race?**
   A. 1989
   B. 1988
   C. 1991
   D. 1990

3. **Who was the first NASCAR Winston Cup championship car owner?**
   A. Jack Roush
   B. Raymond Parks
   C. Carl Kiekhaefer
   D. Rick Hendrick

4. **Who was the 1989 NASCAR Winston Cup Series champion?**
   A. Darrell Waltrip
   B. Bobby Labonte
   C. Dale Earnhardt
   D. Rusty Wallace

5. **What state is Ricky Craven from?**
   A. New Hampshire
   B. Maine
   C. Florida
   D. Delaware

6. **Which driver holds the record for the most NASCAR Winston Cup race wins (fifteen) at Martinsville Speedway?**
   A. Richard Petty
   B. Darrell Waltrip
   C. Cale Yarborough
   D. Dale Earnhardt

7. **What year did Martinsville Speedway celebrate its fiftieth anniversary?**
   A. 1997
   B. 1984
   C. 1995
   D. 1994

8. **The NASCAR Winston Cup Series is the oldest division in NASCAR.**
   A. True
   B. False

9. **What is the oldest division in NASCAR?**
   A. NASCAR Winston Cup Series
   B. NASCAR Busch Series
   C. NASCAR Featherlite Modified Tour
   D. NASCAR Convertible Division

10. **What model of car did Chevrolet race prior to the Monte Carlo?**
    A. Corvette
    B. Camaro
    C. Lumina
    D. S-10

11. **What is Terry Labonte's best-known nickname?**
    A. Powderpuff
    B. Heavy Foot
    C. Iceman
    D. Mouth

12. **Where was Michael Waltrip's first win in a NASCAR Winston Cup car?**
    A. Talladega Superspeedway
    B. Daytona International Speedway
    C. Bristol Motor Speedway
    D. Charlotte Motor Speedway

13. **When Bill Elliott was injured in 1996, who did he choose to be his replacement driver until his return?**
    A. Ricky Craven
    B. Todd Bodine
    C. Greg Sacks
    D. Robert Pressley

14. Who won the first NASCAR-sanctioned race at Martinsville in 1949?
   A. Jim Roper
   B. LeeRoy Yarborough
   C. Red Byron
   D. Marshall Teague

15. Which driver holds the Martinsville Speedway qualifying speed record of 94.129 mph?
   A. Sterling Marlin
   B. Ted Musgrave
   C. Curtis Turner
   D. Fred Lorenzen

16. When a driver reports a "loose" condition in the car, what is he referring to?
   A. Front tires lose grip with the asphalt before the rear tires do.
   B. Rear tires lose grip with the asphalt before the front tires do.
   C. The car pulls to one direction.
   D. The brakes have failed.

17. What is the optimum operating temperature for NASCAR Winston Cup racing tires?
   A. 225 degrees Fahrenheit
   B. 300 degrees Fahrenheit
   C. 12 degrees Celsius
   D. 150 degrees Fahrenheit

18. Who is the only driver to win a NASCAR Winston Cup race with an automatic transmission?
   A. No one
   B. Buddy Baker
   C. Wendall Scott
   D. Tim Flock

19. Why must NASCAR drive shafts be painted white?
   A. to enhance appearance
   B. to make them easier to be seen
   C. to increase durability
   D. so mechanics cannot tell one from the other

20. In NASCAR lingo, what is a donut?
   A. the extra weight around the midsection of a person
   B. a pastry
   C. black circular dents found on the sides of cars after rubbing
   D. a rookie crew chief

21. What year was Martinsville Speedway paved?
   A. 1955
   B. 1960
   C. 1965
   D. 1970

22. True or false: According to NASCAR rules, each NASCAR Winston Cup car preparing to qualify for a race must be completely full of fuel.
   A. True
   B. False

23. What is meant when referring to camber of a tire?
   A. air pressure
   B. amount of resistance shocks
   C. upright angle at which your front tires rest in reference to the road
   D. This term is not used.

24. The movie The Last American Hero was filmed at Martinsville Speedway. It was based on the life of which NASCAR driver?
   A. Richard Petty
   B. Junior Johnson
   C. "Fireball" Roberts
   D. Buddy Baker

25. What is the distance of Martinsville Speedway?
 A. .498 mile
 B. .526 mile
 C. .750 mile
 D. 1.5 miles

26. What driver holds the record for most NASCAR Winston Cup Series poles (eight) at Martinsville Speedway?
 A. Leonard Wood
 B. Michael Waltrip
 C. Darrell Waltrip
 D. Ricky Rudd

27. What is used to inflate the tires on NASCAR Winston Cup cars?
 A. Nitrogen
 B. Oxygen
 C. Hydrogen
 D. Carbon dioxide

28. Who won the first 500-mile race at Martinsville Speedway?
 A. Junior Johnson
 B. Lee Petty
 C. Richard Petty
 D. Buck Baker

29. What company designed and manufactures the NASCAR Racing 2 racing game for personal computers?
 A. 3D
 B. Microsoft
 C. Imagine
 D. Sierra

30. **What is the standard number of cars eligible to start a NASCAR Winston Cup Series race?**
   A. thirty-eight
   B. forty-three
   C. fifty
   D. twenty-four

31. **What year did Cale Yarborough score his first NASCAR Winston Cup victory?**
   A. 1948
   B. 1956
   C. 1965
   D. 1971

32. **What driver has finished second in the Hanes 500 race at Martinsville Speedway four times but has never won a race there?**
   A. Bobby Allison
   B. Richard Petty
   C. Geoff Bodine
   D. Morgan Shepard

33. **Who is the only NASCAR Winston Cup Series driver to win four consecutive Goody's 500 races at Martinsville Speedway?**
   A. Darrell Waltrip
   B. Richard Petty
   C. Cale Yarborough
   D. Rusty Wallace

34. **Who is the only driver to win both the Goody's 500 and the Hanes 500 races in a single season at Martinsville Speedway three times?**
   A. Rusty Wallace
   B. Geoff Bodine
   C. Fred Lorenzen
   D. Richard Petty

35. What NASCAR driver was the first to make the field for an Indy 500 race?
    A. Ken Schrader
    B. Mark Martin
    C. Marshall Teague
    D. Robby Gordon

BONUS QUESTIONS

36. What type of engine is in NASCAR Winston Cup Series cars?
    A. V-8 small block
    B. V-8 large block
    C. V-12
    D. V-6

37. What is the approximate cost of a set of four Goodyear racing tires?
    A. $2,000
    B. $500
    C. $1,300
    D. $1,000

Are you ready to go from the smallest track on the circuit to the biggest? On to Talladega . . .

Martinsville Speedway ticket information:
    (540) 956-3151

Martinsville Speedway

//////NASCAR. SCORECARD

1	2	3	4	5
6	7	8	9	10
11	12	13	14	15
16	17	18	19	20
21	22	23	24	25
26	27	28	29	30
31	32	33	34	35
BONUS 36	BONUS 37			
	TOTAL			

TALLADEGA SUPERSPEEDWAY

Talladega, Alabama

Welcome to Alabama. This is the longest track on the NASCAR Winston Cup circuit. It is a tri-oval superspeedway and is super fast. You have a restrictor plate on your car that will make the competition pretty close. You will also be reaching high speeds, so concentrate and drive smart.

1. The fastest lap ever recorded in a NASCAR Winston Cup Series car was at Talladega Superspeedway. What was the speed?

A. 187.103 mph
B. 200.000 mph

C. 212.809 mph
D. 225.765 mph

2. Which driver set this record?
  A. Dale Earnhardt
  B. Bill Elliott
  C. Dale Jarrett
  D. Bobby Labonte

3. What type of car was he in?
  A. Chevrolet Monte Carlo
  B. Chevrolet Lumina
  C. Pontiac Grand Prix
  D. Ford Thunderbird

4. Which NASCAR Winston Cup Series season had the most races?
  A. 1967
  B. 1974
  C. 1964
  D. 1982

5. How many races were raced that season?
  A. sixty-two
  B. fifty-six
  C. thirty-one
  D. forty-four

6. What was the original name of Talladega Superspeedway?
  A. Alabama International Motor Speedway
  B. Talladega International Motor Speedway
  C. Alabama Raceway
  D. The Speedway

7. What year did Talladega Superspeedway open?
  A. 1972
  B. 1991
  C. 1969
  D. 1953

8. Who won the 1952 NASCAR Manufacturers Cup?
    A. Plymouth
    B. Hudson
    C. Ford
    D. Buick

9. What company owns Talladega Superspeedway?
    A. Speedway Motorsports
    B. International Speedway Corporation
    C. Penske Motorsports
    D. Professional Racing Series

10. Who was the first man to run a closed course at 200 mph in 1970?
    A. Buddy Baker
    B. Bill Elliott
    C. David Pearson
    D. Bobby Allison

11. Which woman has the most NASCAR Winston Cup starts (thirty-three)?
    A. Sara Christian
    B. Janet Guthrie
    C. Patty Moise
    D. Louise Smith

12. Who was known as "the Golden Boy" in NASCAR Winston Cup racing?
    A. Tiny Lund
    B. Jeff Gordon
    C. Joe Weatherly
    D. Fred Lorenzen

13. Who earned his first Talladega Superspeedway win in 1995?
    A. Dale Earnhardt
    B. Sterling Marlin
    C. Dale Jarrett
    D. Michael Waltrip

14. How long is Talladega Superspeedway?
   A. 1.0 miles
   B. 1.76 miles
   C. 2.5 miles
   D. 2.66 miles

15. The banking in the turns at Talladega Superspeedway is how many degrees?
   A. thirty-three
   B. thirty-one
   C. fourteen
   D. twenty-four

16. What manufacturer finished second to Chevrolet in the 1984 through 1989 NASCAR Winston Cup seasons?
   A. Buick
   B. Ford
   C. Dodge
   D. Pontiac

17. Restrictor plates are used at Talladega Superspeedway and which other NASCAR Winston Cup Series race track?
   A. North Carolina Speedway
   B. Darlington Raceway
   C. Daytona International Speedway
   D. Martinsville Speedway

18. When Bill Elliott drove the Coors-sponsored Thunderbird in 1986, what was his number?
   A. five
   B. forty-three
   C. ninety-four
   D. nine

19. What car owner's cars finished first, second, and third in the 1997 Daytona 500?
   A. Robert Yates
   B. Rick Hendrick
   C. Richard Childress
   D. Jack Roush

20. What museum is located at Talladega Superspeedway?
   A. Daytona USA
   B. Mark Martin's Klassix Museum
   C. International Motorsports Hall of Fame and Museum
   D. NASCAR Cafe

21. What family is considered the leader of "the Alabama Gang"?
   A. the Pettys
   B. the Burtons
   C. the Earnhardts
   D. the Allisons

22. Who is the only NASCAR Winston Cup driver to win three consecutive Winston 500 races at Talladega Superspeedway?
   A. David Pearson
   B. Richard Petty
   C. Dale Earnhardt
   D. Bill Elliott

23. How many drivers have won the NASCAR Winston Cup Series championship seven times?
   A. one
   B. two
   C. three
   D. four

24. What driver won the first NASCAR Winston Cup Series race run at Talladega Superspeedway in 1969?
   A. Pete Hamilton
   B. Buddy Baker
   C. Richard Brickhouse
   D. Cale Yarborough

25. What type of car was he driving?
   A. Dodge
   B. Ford
   C. Plymouth
   D. Mercury

26. Which driver holds the record for the most NASCAR Winston Cup Series race wins at Talladega?
   A. Buddy Baker
   B. Jeff Gordon
   C. Dale Earnhardt
   D. Ernie Irvan

27. Who won his only NASCAR Winston Cup race at Talladega Superspeedway in 1988?
   A. Bobby Allison
   B. Terry Labonte
   C. Bill Elliott
   D. Phil Parsons

28. Talladega Superspeedway has the longest grandstands of any track on the NASCAR Winston Cup circuit. How long are they?
   A. 5,280 feet
   B. 2,640 feet
   C. 4,600 feet
   D. 3,020 feet

29. What driver won the inaugural spring NASCAR Winston Cup race (currently called the Winston 500) at Talladega Superspeedway?
   A. Pete Hamilton
   B. Cale Yarborough
   C. David Pearson
   D. Bobby Isaac

30. The start/finish line at Talladega is where?
   A. on the back stretch
   B. in the center of the tri-oval
   C. past the tri-oval
   D. in between turns one and two

31. Who holds the record for the most poles (eight) at Talladega?
   A. Bill Elliott
   B. Jeff Gordon
   C. Geoff Bodine
   D. Dale Jarrett

32. How many pit stalls are there for NASCAR Winston Cup cars at Talladega Superspeedway?
   A. forty
   B. thirty-eight
   C. forty-four
   D. forty-six

33. What NASCAR Winston Cup driver has the most pole wins (four) in the Winston 500 at Talladega?
   A. Bill Elliott
   B. Darrell Waltrip
   C. Cale Yarborough
   D. Dale Earnhardt

34. How many bonus points does a driver receive for leading at least one lap in a NASCAR Winston Cup race?
   A. zero
   B. ten

C. five
D. fifteen

35. What degree is the banking on the back stretch at Talladega Superspeedway?
A. twelve
B. eight
C. five
D. two

BONUS QUESTIONS

36. Who was the first NASCAR Winston Cup driver to drive a Chevrolet to victory at Talladega Superspeedway?
A. Donnie Allison
B. Dale Earnhardt
C. Darrell Waltrip
D. Cale Yarborough

37. Four drivers have won both NASCAR Winston Cup races in one season at Talladega Superspeedway. Which of the following is not one of them?
A. Pete Hamilton
B. Richard Petty
C. Dale Earnhardt
D. Buddy Baker

See you in sunny California . . .

Talladega Superspeedway ticket information:
(256) 362-9064

— 7 2 —

Talladega Superspeedway

NASCAR SCORECARD

1	2	3	4	5
6	7	8	9	10
11	12	13	14	15
16	17	18	19	20
21	22	23	24	25
26	27	28	29	30
31	32	33	34	35
BONUS 36	BONUS 37			

TOTAL

Answer Key for Chapter Eight

1. C	2. B	3. D	4. C	5. A
6. A	7. C	8. B	9. B	
10. A	11. B	12. D	13. B	14. D
15. A	16. B	17. C	18. D	
19. B	20. C	21. D	22. A	23. B
24. C	25. A	26. C	27. D	
28. A	29. A	30. C	31. A	32. D
33. A	34. C	35. D	36. C	
37. B				

CALIFORNIA SPEEDWAY

Fontana, California

Here we are, the ninth race of the season. What better place to be than sunny southern California! Even though California Speedway is brand-new, the racing history in this state is immense. You're almost halfway through the season—so it's time to get down to business. Strap in and earn as many points as you can.

1. What racing legend owns California Speedway?
   A. Richard Petty
   B. Bill France
   C. Roger Penske
   D. Mario Andretti

2. Which NASCAR Winston Cup Series team does he own?

A. #25 Budweiser Chevrolet
B. #2 Miller Lite Ford
C. #28 Havoline Ford
D. #43 STP Pontiac

3. Who won the inaugural NASCAR Winston Cup race at the California Speedway, in 1997?

A. Rusty Wallace
B. John Andretti
C. Ken Schrader
D. Jeff Gordon

4. How steep are the turns banked at California Speedway?

A. fourteen degrees
B. thirty-one degrees
C. twenty-four degrees
D. eighteen degrees

5. What NASCAR Winston Cup driver won the inaugural International Race of Champions (IROC) race at California Speedway?

A. Dale Earnhardt
B. Mark Martin
C. Terry Labonte
D. Robby Gordon

6. In 1984, Terry Labonte clinched his first NASCAR Winston Cup Series championship at which California race track?

A. Ontario Speedway
B. California Speedway
C. Riverside International Raceway
D. Sears Point International Raceway

7. In what year did a Mercury last win a NASCAR Winston Cup race?

A. 1969
B. 1980

C. 1984
D. 1992

8. **How many points does a driver in the NASCAR Winston Cup Series win for finishing second in a race?**
   A. 175
   B. 170
   C. 150
   D. 140

9. **True or false: California Speedway held the first NASCAR Winston Cup event in the state of California.**
   A. True
   B. False

10. **What is the banking on the back stretch at California Speedway?**
    A. twenty-one degrees
    B. sixteen degrees
    C. eight degrees
    D. three degrees

11. **When was the first NASCAR race held at Riverside International Raceway?**
    A. 1978
    B. 1950
    C. 1980
    D. 1958

12. **How many spark plugs are used in a NASCAR Winston Cup engine?**
    A. two
    B. four
    C. six
    D. eight

13. What driver won the first NASCAR race at Riverside (California) International Raceway?
   A. Eddie Gray
   B. Lee Petty
   C. Richard Petty
   D. Junior Johnson

14. Who posted fourteen poles in the 1980 NASCAR Winston Cup season?
   A. Ricky Rudd
   B. Davey Allison
   C. Cale Yarborough
   D. Dale Earnhardt

15. What driver won the 1958 NASCAR Winston Cup race at Sacramento Fairgrounds?
   A. Ron Hornaday
   B. Parnelli Jones
   C. Bob Price
   D. "Fireball" Roberts

16. What two drivers are the only seven-time NASCAR Winston Cup Series champions?
   A. Dale Earnhardt and Darrell Waltrip
   B. Dale Earnhardt and Richard Petty
   C. Richard Petty and Lee Petty
   D. Richard Petty and Cale Yarborough

17. How long was Riverside International Raceway?
   A. 1.5 miles
   B. 2.0 miles
   C. 2.216 miles
   D. 2.631 miles

18. How long is California Speedway?
   A. 1.5 miles
   B. 2.0 miles
   C. 1.0 miles
   D. 2.5 miles

19. When was the last NASCAR Winston Cup race held at Riverside, California?
    A. 1988
    B. 1986
    C. 1990
    D. 1989

20. Who won the last NASCAR Winston Cup race at Riverside?
    A. Dale Earnhardt
    B. Rusty Wallace
    C. Dick Trickle
    D. Davey Allison

21. The last race at Ontario (California) Motor Speedway was held in what year?
    A. 1981
    B. 1977
    C. 1972
    D. 1980

22. Who won the last race at Ontario Motor Speedway?
    A. Neil Bonnett
    B. Benny Parsons
    C. Dale Earnhardt
    D. Bobby Allison

23. What NASCAR driver wrapped up the 1980 NASCAR Winston Cup championship at that race?
    A. Dale Earnhardt
    B. Cale Yarborough
    C. Terry Labonte
    D. Richard Petty

24. What year was the first NASCAR Winston Cup race run at Ontario Motor Speedway?
    A. 1969
    B. 1975
    C. 1971
    D. 1957

25. Who won that first race at Ontario Motor Speedway?
    A. A. J. Foyt
    B. Bobby Isaac
    C. Elmo Langley
    D. Marv Acton

26. At what track did the NASCAR Winston Cup Series celebrate its 1000th race?
    A. California Motor Speedway
    B. Ontario Motor Speedway
    C. Sacramento Fairgrounds
    D. Riverside International Raceway

27. Tires that have not been used are referred to as what type of tires?
    A. sticker tires
    B. scuffed tires
    C. grooved tires
    D. Petty tires

28. The first NASCAR race in California was held at what track?
    A. Oakland Stadium
    B. Carrell Speedway
    C. Riverside International Raceway
    D. Laguna Seca Raceway

29. What year was that race held?
    A. 1949
    B. 1957
    C. 1951
    D. 1982

30. NASCAR has raced in many cities in California. Which of the following is not one of them?
    A. Riverside
    B. Eureka
    C. Sacramento
    D. Laguna Hills

---

31. In what year was Riverside International Raceway the first and last stop on the NASCAR Winston Cup Series schedule?
   A. 1967
   B. 1990
   C. 1972
   D. 1981

32. How many valve stems do NASCAR tires have?
   A. one
   B. two
   C. three
   D. four

33. Who was the first NASCAR Winston Cup Series driver from the state of Tennessee to win Rookie of the Year honors (1983)?
   A. Bobby Hamilton
   B. John Andretti
   C. Sterling Marlin
   D. Johnny Benson

34. Who won the only NASCAR Winston Cup race ever held in Iowa (1953)?
   A. Buddy Baker
   B. Hershell McGriff
   C. Donnie Allison
   D. Herb Thomas

35. What size are the wheels on NASCAR Winston Cup cars?
   A. fifteen inches
   B. fourteen inches
   C. seventeen inches
   D. sixteen inches

BONUS QUESTIONS

36. What driver was seventeen years old and still in high school when he raced in his first NASCAR Winston Cup Series race?
   A. Bobby Hillin
   B. Jeff Burton
   C. Dale Earnhardt
   D. Jeff Gordon

37. Which of the following drivers has never been voted the NASCAR Winston Cup Most Popular Driver?
   A. Bill Elliott
   B. Geoff Bodine
   C. Darrell Waltrip
   D. David Pearson

Yet another cross-country trip! On to Charlotte Motor Speedway . . .

California Speedway ticket information:
   (800) 944-RACE (7223)

///////NASCAR® SCORECARD

1	**2**	**3**	**4**	**5**
6	**7**	**8**	**9**	**10**
11	**12**	**13**	**14**	**15**
16	**17**	**18**	**19**	**20**
21	**22**	**23**	**24**	**25**
26	**27**	**28**	**29**	**30**
31	**32**	**33**	**34**	**35**
BONUS **36**	BONUS **37**			

TOTAL

Answer Key to Chapter Nine

1. C 2. B 3. D 4. A 5. B 6. C 7. B 8. B 9. B
10. D 11. D 12. D 13. A 14. C 15. B 16. B 17. D 18. B
19. A 20. B 21. D 22. B 23. A 24. C 25. A 26. B 27. A
28. B 29. C 30. D 31. D 32. B 33. C 34. D 35. A 36. A
37. B

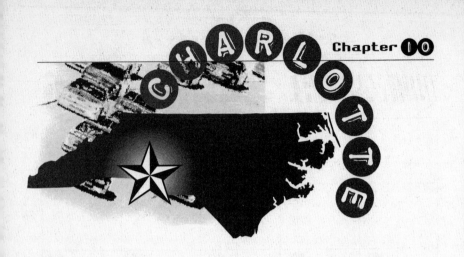

Chapter 10

CHARLOTTE MOTOR SPEEDWAY

Concord, North Carolina

Welcome to North Carolina. You're at the halfway point of the season and halfway to the NASCAR Championship. Charlotte Motor Speedway is host to NASCAR's longest race, so endurance will be a factor here. Stay alert and stay out in front; you'll need the points!

1. **Which two drivers have the most NASCAR Winston Cup Series wins (six) at Charlotte Motor Speedway?**
   A. Dale Earnhardt and Bobby Allison
   B. Curtis Turner and Richard Petty
   C. Bobby Allison and Darrell Waltrip
   D. "Fireball" Roberts and David Pearson

2. **Who holds the near-untouchable record for pole wins (fourteen) at Charlotte?**
   A. David Pearson
   B. Fred Lorenzen
   C. Benny Parsons
   D. Marvin Panch

3. **What was the inaugural year of the Winston (the NASCAR Winston Cup Series All-Star event)?**
   A. 1979
   B. 1983
   C. 1985
   D. 1994

4. **What year was Jeff Gordon the NASCAR Winston Cup Series Rookie of the Year?**
   A. 1989
   B. 1991
   C. 1993
   D. 1995

5. **How many wins did Darrell Waltrip have in the 1982 NASCAR Winston Cup season?**
   A. five
   B. eight
   C. ten
   D. twelve

6. **What driver has not won the Coca-Cola 600 race two consecutive times?**
   A. Dale Earnhardt
   B. Richard Petty
   C. Darrell Waltrip
   D. Neil Bonnett

7. Several drivers have won each of the two NASCAR Winston Cup Series races at Charlotte Motor Speedway in a single season. Which of the following has not?
A. David Pearson
B. Darrell Waltrip
C. Bobby Allison
D. Fred Lorenzen

8. Since the inception of the Winston, which year was it held at Atlanta Motor Speedway and not Charlotte Motor Speedway?
A. 1979
B. 1984
C. 1986
D. 1992

9. Charlotte Motor Speedway is how long?
A. 1.5 miles
B. 2.0 miles
C. 2.34 miles
D. 2.66 miles

10. Who was the winner of the first NASCAR Winston Cup Series race at Charlotte Motor Speedway, in 1960?
A. Speedy Thompson
B. Joe Weatherly
C. Joe Lee Johnson
D. Nelson Stacy

11. Who is second on the all-time NASCAR Winston Cup win list?
A. David Pearson
B. Dale Earnhardt
C. Bill Elliott
D. Cale Yarborough

---

12. What was the first year a 600-mile race was run at Charlotte Motor Speedway?
   A. 1960
   B. 1959
   C. 1954
   D. 1948

13. In the 1960 World 600 race at Charlotte Motor Speedway, car owner Bud Moore tried to stop a leaking fuel cell by using what to plug the hole?
   A. putty
   B. a paper towel
   C. duct tape
   D. a bar of soap

14. Who was the first NASCAR Winston Cup Series driver to top $10 million in career winnings?
   A. Richard Petty
   B. Dale Earnhardt
   C. Darrell Waltrip
   D. Bill Elliott

15. What year did he top $10 million?
   A. 1989
   B. 1988
   C. 1990
   D. 1991

16. What make of car did Richard Petty drive to victory twice in 1975 at Charlotte Motor Speedway?
   A. Pontiac
   B. Buick
   C. Dodge
   D. Plymouth

17. How many NASCAR Winston Cup races were won in a Studebaker?
   A. three
   B. seven
   C. ten
   D. twenty-five

18. In what year did David Pearson reach 100 NASCAR Winston Cup victories?
   A. 1972
   B. 1978
   C. 1981
   D. 1980

19. What year did Darrell Waltrip win his first NASCAR Winston Cup race?
   A. 1969
   B. 1972
   C. 1975
   D. 1981

20. Where did Darrell Waltrip's first NASCAR Winston Cup victory occur?
   A. Daytona Beach, Florida
   B. Nashville, Tennessee
   C. Raleigh, North Carolina
   D. Columbia, South Carolina

21. Who was the first driver to race in the Indianapolis 500 and the Charlotte 600 on the same day?
   A. Robby Gordon
   B. A. J. Foyt
   C. John Andretti
   D. Dan Gurney

22. What year did he accomplish this?
   A. 1994
   B. 1992
   C. 1977
   D. 1997

---

23. What year did David Pearson win his last NASCAR Winston Cup Series race?
A. 1977
B. 1980
C. 1982
D. 1984

24. How many NASCAR Winston Cup victories did he have in his career?
A. 100
B. 102
C. 105
D. 110

25. How many wins did Darrell Waltrip have in his 1985 NASCAR Winston Cup Series championship season?
A. two
B. three
C. seven
D. eleven

26. In that same season, how many wins did Bill Elliott (who finished second to Waltrip) have?
A. two
B. three
C. seven
D. eleven

27. What year did Cale Yarborough retire from driving?
A. 1978
B. 1984
C. 1988
D. 1990

28. Who holds the track speed record of 185.759 mph at Charlotte Motor Speedway?
   A. Hut Stricklin
   B. Ward Burton
   C. Mike Skinner
   D. Mark Martin

29. What does the black flag in NASCAR racing mean?
   A. caution
   B. stop
   C. one lap to go
   D. report to the pits immediately

30. In the 1967 NASCAR Winston Cup Series, how many victories did Richard Petty have?
   A. seventeen
   B. twenty
   C. twenty-two
   D. twenty-seven

31. When was the first NASCAR Winston Cup Series road race held?
   A. 1954
   B. 1959
   C. 1965
   D. 1982

32. Where was that race held?
   A. Watkins Glen International Raceway
   B. Linden (New Jersey) Airport
   C. Riverside International Raceway
   D. Detroit Airport

33. What driver won that race?
   A. "Fireball" Roberts
   B. Joe Eubanks
   C. Lee Petty
   D. Al Keller

34. What year did Richard Petty retire as a driver?
   A. 1988
   B. 1989
   C. 1992
   D. 1994

35. What did he call his tour that year?
   A. Good-bye Richard Tour
   B. King Richard's Farewell Tour
   C. Petty Enterprises Tour
   D. Fan Appreciation Tour

BONUS QUESTIONS

36. What year did Jeff Gordon win his first NASCAR Winston Cup Championship?
   A. 1997
   B. 1995
   C. 1991
   D. 1994

37. Who won his first NASCAR Winston Cup race at Charlotte Motor Speedway?
   A. Dale Earnhardt
   B. Rusty Wallace
   C. Jeff Gordon
   D. Dale Jarrett

You're halfway there. Dover Downs is next...

Charlotte Motor Speedway ticket information:
   (704) 455-3200

///////NASCAR. SCORECARD

1	2	3	4	5
6	7	8	9	10
11	12	13	14	15
16	17	18	19	20
21	22	23	24	25
26	27	28	29	30
31	32	33	34	35
BONUS 36	BONUS 37			
		TOTAL		

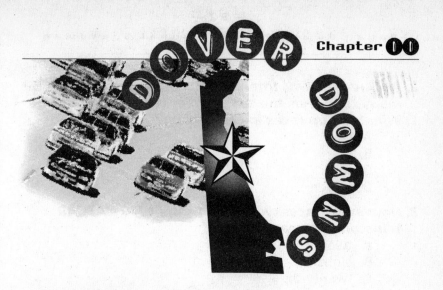

Chapter 11

DOVER DOWNS INTERNATIONAL SPEEDWAY

Dover, Delaware

Welcome to Dover Downs. You've learned a lot already in your rookie season, but now it's time to focus on your car. Here you'll find a few questions concerning NASCAR slang and car setup. The racing is basic, but remember to always keep your eyes open.

1. What driver won both NASCAR Winston Cup races at Dover Downs International Speedway in 1996?
   A. Rusty Wallace
   B. Ricky Rudd
   C. Jeff Gordon
   D. Dale Earnhardt

2. At Dover Downs International Speedway, how many times has the same driver won both NASCAR Winston Cup races in one season?
   A. two
   B. five
   C. six
   D. eleven

3. How many races were held in the 1949 NASCAR Winston Cup season?
   A. two
   B. eight
   C. twenty-six
   D. thirty-two

4. What is the pit road speed limit at Dover?
   A. 15 mph
   B. 25 mph
   C. 35 mph
   D. 55 mph

5. At each NASCAR Winston Cup race every car is weighed. NASCAR scales can tell not only a car's weight, but also how that weight is distributed. What is the maximum weight one side of the car can have?
   A. 1900 pounds
   B. 2000 pounds
   C. 3500 pounds
   D. 2500 pounds

6. What does the term wedge mean?
   A. shock resistance
   B. spoiler height
   C. adjusting the car's weight at each wheel
   D. something the pit crew does to the driver after winning the race

7. What does the term marbles mean?
   A. a crew chief has made a bad decision
   B. the loose rubber that collects in the upper groove of the race track

    C. the pieces of asphalt that get caught in the tires

    D. there are marbles on the race track

8. What type of transmission is located in NASCAR Winston Cup stock cars?

    A. automatic

    B. five-speed

    C. three-speed

    D. four-speed

9. Who is the winningest car owner in Dover Downs history (six wins)?

    A. Felix Sabates

    B. Junior Johnson

    C. Wood Brothers

    D. Richard Childress

10. Richard Petty won the first NASCAR race at Dover Downs, the Mason-Dixon 300, in 1969 driving what kind of car?

    A. Buick

    B. Chevrolet

    C. Ford

    D. Pontiac

11. Who is the only driver to win three NASCAR Winston Cup races at Dover Downs from the pole position?

    A. Dale Earnhardt

    B. Bobby Allison

    C. David Pearson

    D. Cale Yarborough

12. Head wrench *is NASCAR slang for what?*

    A. team owner

    B. crew chief

    C. driver

    D. engine builder

13. How many lug nuts hold on each tire of a NASCAR Winston Cup stock car?
A. six
B. one
C. five
D. four

14. Which driver holds the record for the most poles (six) at Dover Downs?
A. Ricky Rudd
B. Alan Kulwicki
C. David Pearson
D. Jeff Gordon

15. Who is credited with coming up with the current NASCAR Winston Cup point system?
A. Richard Petty
B. Bob Latford
C. Bill France
D. ESPN

16. Dover Downs was the first NASCAR superspeedway to use what on the track?
A. asphalt
B. cement
C. concrete
D. rubber

17. How many divisions does NASCAR sanction?
A. twelve
B. three
C. two
D. one

18. Bobby Labonte holds the Dover Downs track qualifying speed record. How fast did he run?
A. 155.086 mph
B. 158.980 mph
C. 160.546 mph
D. 175.362 mph

19. Which two drivers share the record for the most NASCAR Winston Cup wins (seven) at Dover Downs?
    A. Jeff Gordon and Bill Elliott
    B. Bobby Allison and Richard Petty
    C. Dale Earnhardt and David Pearson
    D. Bobby Allison and Bill Elliott

20. The straightaways at Dover are banked at what angle?
    A. two degrees
    B. five degrees
    C. nine degrees
    D. twelve degrees

21. What is the last practice session before a NASCAR Winston Cup race known as?
    A. last practice
    B. last chance
    C. happy hour
    D. midnight special

22. What brand of fuel is used in all NASCAR Winston Cup Series cars?
    A. Exxon
    B. Hess
    C. Chevron
    D. 76

23. Who was the first African-American to run in a NASCAR Winston Cup race?
    A. Wendell Scott
    B. Richard Pryor
    C. Joie Ray
    D. Scott Thomas

24. What is the minimum height requirement for the car numbers on NASCAR stock cars?
    A. no requirement
    B. eighteen inches
    C. ten inches
    D. thirty inches

25. How many miles was the first NASCAR race at Dover Downs in 1969?
    A. 250
    B. 300
    C. 400
    D. 500

26. Dover Downs is also known as what?
    A. The Monster Mile
    B. The Grand One
    C. The Track Too Tough to Tame
    D. The Black Widow

27. True or false: The second NASCAR Winston Cup Series race at Dover Downs each year is the NASCAR Winston Cup Series' final stop in the Northeast.
    A. True
    B. False

28. Jeff Gordon won three consecutive NASCAR Winston Cup Series races at Dover Downs. Which other two drivers have also accomplished this?
    A. Dale Earnhardt and Richard Petty
    B. David Pearson and Rusty Wallace
    C. Lee Petty and Darrell Waltrip
    D. Harry Gant and Neil Bonnett

29. True or false: NASCAR Winston Cup cars have speedometers.
    A. True
    B. False

30. How many provisional starting spots are available in each NASCAR Winston Cup race?
A. three
B. five
C. seven
D. one

31. In 1996 Jeff Gordon swept both NASCAR Winston Cup Series races at Dover Downs. What driver also swept both NASCAR Busch Series races that same year?
A. Steve Park
B. Hermie Sadler
C. Kevin Lapage
D. Randy LaJoie

32. What type of track is located on the inside of Dover Downs?
A. dog track
B. horse track
C. track-and-field track
D. go-cart track

33. How many gallons of gasoline can a NASCAR Winston Cup gas can hold?
A. five
B. eight
C. eleven
D. twenty-two

34. How much oil do the oil reserve tanks on NASCAR Winston Cup cars hold?
A. ten quarts
B. eighteen quarts
C. five quarts
D. twenty-two quarts

35. How many cars will be guaranteed a starting spot after first-round qualifying for a NASCAR Winston Cup race?
  A. ten
  B. twenty
  C. twenty-five
  D. thirty-eight

BONUS QUESTIONS

36. How many times has a NASCAR Winston Cup race at Dover Downs been won from the pole?
  A. four
  B. eight
  C. ten
  D. twelve

37. How many NASCAR Winston Cup starts did it take Mark Martin to win his first pole?
  A. one
  B. three
  C. seven
  D. fifteen

Just a short trip down the road to Richmond, but a very different race track. See you there...

Dover Downs International Speedway ticket information:
  (800) 441-RACE outside Delaware
  (302) 734-7223 from anywhere

NASCAR. SCORECARD

1	2	3	4	5
6	7	8	9	10
11	12	13	14	15
16	17	18	19	20
21	22	23	24	25
26	27	28	29	30
31	32	33	34	35
BONUS 36	BONUS 37			
	TOTAL			

Chapter 12

RICHMOND INTERNATIONAL RACEWAY

Richmond, Virginia

Richmond International Raceway is one of the oldest tracks on the NASCAR Winston Cup Series circuit, so...yep, you guessed it, lots of history. Your team and your adoring fans are confident that you will do great. You can dazzle them with your skillful racing, just don't forget those valuable points!

1. **What was the first year NASCAR Winston Cup cars raced at Richmond International Raceway?**
   A. 1953
   B. 1958
   C. 1961
   D. 1985

2. **Who has won more NASCAR Winston Cup races (thirteen) at Richmond than any other driver?**
   A. Dale Earnhardt
   B. Richard Petty
   C. Darrell Waltrip
   D. Bobby Allison

3. **When cars sit on pit road prior to a NASCAR Winston Cup Series race they usually have a generator hooked up to them. What is its primary purpose?**
   A. warms up the engine
   B. allows the driver to listen to the radio
   C. provides communication between the driver and crew chief
   D. keeps the oil warm

4. **Who drove the Quality Care Ford prior to Dale Jarrett?**
   A. Ricky Rudd
   B. Geoff Bodine
   C. Dick Trickle
   D. Ernie Irvan

5. **Who has won the Most Popular Driver award the most times (twelve)?**
   A. Richard Petty
   B. Darrell Waltrip
   C. Bobby Allison
   D. Bill Elliott

6. **Who got a NASCAR Winston Cup Series victory first, Ward or Jeff Burton?**
   A. Jeff Burton
   B. Ward Burton

7. **Bill Elliott's 1988 NASCAR Winston Cup championship was the first time Ford had won a championship since what year?**
   A. 1969
   B. 1978
   C. 1985
   D. 1987

8. **What year was the current NASCAR Winston Cup Series point system introduced?**
   A. 1948
   B. 1975
   C. 1978
   D. 1985

9. **Which two drivers have the most NASCAR Winston Cup poles (eight) at Richmond International Raceway?**
   A. Bobby Allison and Darrell Waltrip
   B. Jeff Gordon and Mark Martin
   C. Bobby Allison and Richard Petty
   D. Dale Earnhardt and Richard Petty

10. **Who won the first Winston?**
    A. Darrell Waltrip
    B. Bill Elliott
    C. Dale Earnhardt
    D. Davey Allison

11. **Who is the winningest car owner at Richmond International Raceway?**
    A. Richard Childress
    B. Roger Penske
    C. Richard Petty
    D. Robert Yates

12. You probably know that Bill Elliott is the fastest man in NASCAR, but who is second fastest?
A. Tim Richmond
B. Bobby Allison
C. Herb Thomas
D. Kyle Petty

13. Which NASCAR Winston Cup Series driver once drove a pink race car as a teenager?
A. Dale Earnhardt
B. Buddy Backer
C. Ned Jarrett
D. Dick Trickle

14. What is the fastest lap speed ever recorded at Richmond?
A. 80.696 mph
B. 104.321 mph
C. 124.757 mph
D. 150.536 mph

15. What is the track distance of Richmond?
A. .500 mile
B. .750 mile
C. 1.50 miles
D. 2.00 miles

16. What shape is Richmond International Speedway?
A. tri-oval
B. round
C. pear-shaped
D. D-shaped oval

17. Who determines what paint scheme a car will have?
A. the driver
B. the primary sponsor
C. the car owner
D. NASCAR

18. What happens if a driver fails to attend the drivers' meeting prior to a NASCAR Winston Cup Series race?
    A. nothing
    B. His car is disqualified.
    C. His car starts the race at the back of the pack.
    D. The car owner pays a fine.

19. Which country music star used to race in the NASCAR Winston Cup Series?
    A. Brooks and Dunn
    B. Kenny Rogers
    C. Johnny Cash
    D. Marty Robbins

20. 76 Racing gasoline awards money to a driver if he or she wins a race from the pole. What happens to the money if the pole sitter does not win the race?
    A. It rolls over to the next race.
    B. It is awarded to the winner of the race.
    C. The money is equally distributed among all drivers.
    D. It is added to the next year's Bud Pole Award.

21. How many cars make the field in the second round of qualifying?
    A. ten
    B. eleven
    C. thirteen
    D. forty-two

22. What year did Mark Martin start racing for Jack Roush?
    A. 1982
    B. 1988
    C. 1993
    D. 1994

23. When were body templates introduced?
   A. 1990
   B. 1983
   C. 1977
   D. 1967

24. How many NASCAR Winston Cup Series races are run at Richmond each year?
   A. one
   B. two
   C. three
   D. four

25. What position did Rusty Wallace finish in his first NASCAR Winston Cup Series race?
   A. first
   B. second
   C. eleventh
   D. twenty-second

26. What was the previous name of Richmond International Raceway?
   A. Strawberry Hill Speedway
   B. Virginia Speedway
   C. Atlantic North Speedway
   D. Carnival Raceway

27. Where was Bill France Sr. born in 1909?
   A. New York, New York
   B. Daytona Beach, Florida
   C. Washington, D.C.
   D. Charlotte, North Carolina

28. What driver won the inaugural NASCAR event at Richmond International Raceway, in 1953?
   A. Tom Pistone
   B. Lee Petty
   C. Cotton Owens
   D. Rex White

29. What type of car was he driving?
A. Chevrolet
B. Ford
C. Plymouth
D. Dodge

30. What year was Richmond International Raceway paved?
A. 1945
B. 1950
C. 1968
D. 1975

31. What is the largest field to ever start a NASCAR race (Daytona Beach, 1953)?
A. 43
B. 74
C. 148
D. 161

32. How many NASCAR Winston Cup races were won by a Hudson Hornet?
A. none
B. five
C. forty-six
D. seventy-nine

33. Who was the first NASCAR Winston Cup Driver to win at Richmond International Raceway after it was redesigned?
A. Dale Earnhardt
B. Bill Elliott
C. Ricky Rudd
D. Davey Allison

34. What legendary NASCAR driver did not win the Rookie of the Year title?
A. Richard Petty
B. Darrell Waltrip

   C. Dale Earnhardt
   D. Donnie Allison

35. Does Richmond have back stretch pitting?
   A. Yes
   B. No

BONUS QUESTIONS

36. Which driver won every NASCAR Winston Cup event at Richmond International Raceway from the fall of 1970 to the fall of 1973?
   A. Bobby Allison
   B. David Pearson
   C. Richard Petty
   D. Cale Yarborough

37. How many consecutive wins did he have during that time period?
   A. seven
   B. six
   C. eight
   D. nine

With a dozen races down, concentrate and make sure thirteen is not unlucky for you. Let's head to the Irish Hills of Michigan.

Richmond International Raceway ticket information:
   (804) 345-RACE

|||||||||NASCAR. SCORECARD

1	2	3	4	5
6	**7**	**8**	**9**	**10**
11	**12**	**13**	**14**	**15**
16	**17**	**18**	**19**	**20**
21	**22**	**23**	**24**	**25**
26	**27**	**28**	**29**	**30**
31	**32**	**33**	**34**	**35**
BONUS **36**	BONUS **37**			
	TOTAL			

Answer Key to Chapter Twelve

1. A   2. B   3. D   4. C   5. D   6. B   7. A   8. B   9. C
10. A   11. C   12. B   13. A   14. C   15. B   16. D   17. B   18. C
19. D   20. A   21. B   22. B   23. D   24. B   25. B   26. A   27. C
28. B   29. D   30. C   31. C   32. D   33. D   34. B   35. B   36. C
37. A

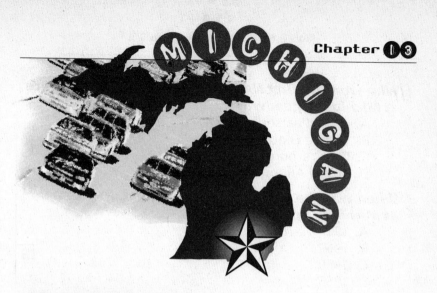

Chapter 13

MICHIGAN SPEEDWAY

Brooklyn, Michigan

Here we are at Michigan Speedway for the thirteenth race of the season. There are two lines around Michigan Speedway: One is at the bottom of the track, the other at the top. Pick your favorite, but the key here is to stay smooth and consistent.

1. **Who designed both the Daytona International Speedway and Michigan Speedway?**
   A. Bill France Sr.
   B. Charles Moneypenny
   C. Roger Penske
   D. Marvin Tutor

2. Who won the first NASCAR Winston Cup Series race at Michigan Speedway?
    A. David Pearson
    B. Charlie Glotzbach
    C. Cale Yarborough
    D. Bobby Allison

3. When was the first NASCAR Winston Cup race held at Michigan Speedway?
    A. 1974
    B. 1969
    C. 1980
    D. 1955

4. What driver started his 1,000th race at Michigan Speedway?
    A. Darrell Waltrip
    B. Richard Petty
    C. Dale Earnhardt
    D. Cale Yarborough

5. What was the name of the track before being named Michigan Speedway?
    A. Greater Detroit Speedway
    B. Michigan Oval
    C. Michigan International Raceway
    D. Michigan Raceway

6. When was the name changed to Michigan Speedway?
    A. 1988
    B. 1996
    C. 1977
    D. 1972

7. What other NASCAR Winston Cup track was almost identically designed after the Michigan Speedway?
    A. California Speedway
    B. North Carolina Speedway
    C. Texas Motor Speedway
    D. Phoenix International Raceway

8. **Which of the following drivers does not reside in North Carolina?**
    A. Jeremy Mayfield
    B. Chad Little
    C. Dale Jarrett
    D. Bobby Hamilton

9. **How long is Michigan Speedway?**
    A. 1.0 miles
    B. 2.0 miles
    C. 2.5 miles
    D. 5 miles

10. **What is the banking in the turns at Michigan Speedway?**
    A. eighteen degrees
    B. twenty degrees
    C. twenty-five degrees
    D. thirty degrees

11. **Which of the following drivers is from Missouri?**
    A. Chad Little
    B. Kenny Wallace
    C. Derrike Cope
    D. Ricky Rudd

12. **What driver has the most NASCAR Winston Cup victories (nine) at Michigan Speedway?**
    A. Cale Yarborough
    B. Buddy Baker
    C. David Pearson
    D. Bill Elliott

13. **What driver got to take a ride in an F-16 in 1987?**
    A. Mark Martin
    B. Bill Elliott
    C. Jeff Gordon
    D. Bobby Labonte

14. How many Rookie of the Year title holders have gone on to win a NASCAR Winston Cup championship?
   A. twenty-three
   B. fifteen
   C. ten
   D. seven

15. What year did Dale Earnhardt's consecutive season win streak end?
   A. 1997
   B. 1996
   C. 1994
   D. 1989

16. If two drivers have the same number of points at the end of the season, what is the tiebreaker?
   A. car owner points
   B. number of race wins that season
   C. highest finish in previous season
   D. most NASCAR Winston Cup starts

17. Where did the first international NASCAR Winston Cup race take place, in 1953?
   A. Germany
   B. Canada
   C. Japan
   D. Mexico

18. Who is the winningest car owner (eleven wins) in Michigan Speedway history?
   A. Melling Racing
   B. Wood Brothers
   C. Junior Johnson
   D. Richard Childress

19. Who won the first NASCAR Winston Cup race ever (1949)?
   A. Joe Weatherly
   B. Red Byron

C. Ralph Earnhardt
D. Jim Roper

20. What year was Darrell Waltrip's twenty-fifth in NASCAR Winston Cup Series competition?
A. 1990
B. 1997
C. 1995
D. 1993

21. From 1971 to 1976, only three NASCAR Winston Cup drivers won at Michigan Speedway. Which of the following was not one of them?
A. Bobby Allison
B. David Pearson
C. Richard Petty
D. Darrell Waltrip

22. Michael Waltrip is originally from what state?
A. Tennessee
B. North Carolina
C. Kentucky
D. Georgia

23. Who has the most NASCAR Winston Cup starts at Michigan Speedway?
A. Mark Martin
B. Donnie Allison
C. Neil Bonnett
D. Dave Marcis

24. What is the banking in the corners at Michigan Speedway?
A. eight degrees
B. eighteen degrees
C. twenty degrees
D. thirty-four degrees

25. Who holds the Michigan Speedway track qualifying speed record (186.611 mph)?
A. Jeff Burton
B. Dale Jarrett
C. Bobby Labonte
D. Jeff Gordon

26. What driver won both of the 1995 NASCAR Winston Cup races at Michigan Speedway?
A. Bobby Labonte
B. Rusty Wallace
C. Dale Jarrett
D. Mark Martin

27. What type of car was he driving?
A. Ford
B. Pontiac
C. Chevrolet
D. Oldsmobile

28. What was the first year the Rookie of the Year award was given?
A. 1948
B. 1958
C. 1966
D. 1992

29. How many NASCAR Winston Cup races have been won from the pole at Michigan?
A. thirteen
B. nine
C. twenty
D. none

30. Who holds the NASCAR Winston Cup record for career winning percentage (21.2%)?
A. Terry Labonte
B. Harry Gant
C. David Pearson
D. Tim Flock

31. How many NASCAR Winston Cup victories were won by the three Flock brothers (Tim, Fonty, and Bob)?
- A. two
- B. nineteen
- C. forty-nine
- D. sixty-two

32. Who was the first multicar team owner?
- A. Robert Yates
- B. Raymond Parks
- C. Carl Keikhaefer
- D. Rick Hendrick

33. What was the first year he had a multicar team?
- A. 1955
- B. 1976
- C. 1983
- D. 1995

34. How many races did his team win that season?
- A. four
- B. twelve
- C. sixteen
- D. twenty-two

35. What shape is Michigan Speedway?
- A. round
- B. tri-oval
- C. D-shaped
- D. perfect oval

BONUS QUESTIONS

36. Who is the only driver to win the Rookie of the Year title in both the NASCAR Winston Cup Series and the NASCAR Busch Series?
   A. Dale Earnhardt
   B. Rusty Wallace
   C. Jeff Gordon
   D. Mike Skinner

37. Who is the oldest driver to win a NASCAR Winston Cup race (age fifty-two)?
   A. Richard Petty
   B. Buddy Baker
   C. Harry Gant
   D. Red Byron

Next stop: the beautiful mountains of Pennsylvania...

Michigan Speedway ticket information:
   (800) 354-1010

//////NASCAR. SCORECARD

1	**2**	**3**	**4**	**5**
6	**7**	**8**	**9**	**10**
11	**12**	**13**	**14**	**15**
16	**17**	**18**	**19**	**20**
21	**22**	**23**	**24**	**25**
26	**27**	**28**	**29**	**30**
31	**32**	**33**	**34**	**35**
BONUS **36**	BONUS **37**	**TOTAL**		

Answer Key for Chapter Thirteen
1. B   2. C   3. B   4. B   5. C   6. B   7. A   8. D   9. B
10. A   11. B   12. C   13. B   14. D   15. A   16. B   17. B   18. B
19. D   20. B   21. D   22. C   23. D   24. B   25. D   26. A   27. C
28. B   29. A   30. D   31. D   32. B   33. A   34. D   35. C   36. C
37. C

Chapter 14

POCONO RACEWAY

Long Pond, Pennsylvania

I t's race time here in the beautiful mountains of Pennsylvania. Don't let the scenery and your mob of fans deter you from your main goal. Pocono is a unique track with three turns, each with a different radius and different degree of banking. Concentrate and pick up as many points as possible.

1. What is the shape of Pocono Raceway?
   A. road course
   B. D-shaped oval
   C. triangle
   D. short track

2. True or false: Fuel injection is allowed in NASCAR Winston Cup cars.
    A. True
    B. False

3. What driver holds the record for most NASCAR Winston Cup dirt track wins (forty-three)?
    A. Herb Thomas
    B. Tim Flock
    C. Buck Baker
    D. Lee Petty

4. What does the black flag with the white stripe mean in NASCAR Winston Cup racing?
    A. stop
    B. the car is not being scored
    C. a car is about to be lapped
    D. a car is disqualified

5. What city is Pocono Raceway located in?
    A. Willow Grove
    B. Pax River
    C. Long Pond
    D. Quiet Valley

6. What does the white flag mean in NASCAR Winston Cup racing?
    A. report to the pits immediately
    B. slower car on the track
    C. one lap to go
    D. use caution

7. What is the distance of Pocono Raceway?
    A. 1.5 miles
    B. 2.0 miles
    C. 2.5 miles
    D. 3.0 miles

8. In NASCAR Winston Cup racing, who is assigned the car number?
  A. the driver
  B. the crew chief
  C. the manufacturer
  D. the car owner

9. Who is the only driver to win at Pocono driving an Oldsmobile?
  A. Bobby Allison
  B. Rusty Wallace
  C. Darrell Waltrip
  D. Harry Gant

10. During a pit stop, who usually cleans off the grille?
  A. the front tire changer
  B. the front tire carrier
  C. the driver
  D. the fuel person

11. When was the first NASCAR Winston Cup race held at Pocono Raceway?
  A. 1982
  B. 1974
  C. 1968
  D. 1991

12. NASCAR's official Web site is located at what address?
  A. www.racing.com
  B. www.fastcars.com
  C. www.nascar.com
  D. www.winston.com

13. What driver won the first NASCAR Winston Cup race at Pocono Raceway?
  A. Bobby Allison
  B. David Pearson
  C. Rusty Wallace
  D. Richard Petty

14. Who was Jeff Gordon's crew chief in 1997?
   A. Rick Hendrick
   B. Brad Parrott
   C. Ray Evernham
   D. Jimmy Makar

15. Three NASCAR Winston Cup drivers have won back-to-back races at Pocono Raceway. Which of the following is not one of them?
   A. Dale Earnhardt
   B. Bill Elliott
   C. Bobby Allison
   D. Tim Richmond

16. In which of the following NASCAR Winston Cup seasons did Dale Earnhardt not win a race?
   A. 1980
   B. 1992
   C. 1981
   D. 1988

17. Who has sat on the pole the most times (five) at Pocono Raceway?
   A. Ernie Irvan
   B. Joe Nemechek
   C. Bill Elliott
   D. Ken Schrader

18. Who was the 1989 NASCAR Winston Cup runner-up?
   A. Dale Earnhardt
   B. Rusty Wallace
   C. Darrell Waltrip
   D. Terry Labonte

19. What NASCAR Winston Cup driver won both races at Pocono Raceway in 1986?
   A. Geoff Bodine
   B. Harry Gant
   C. Darrell Waltrip
   D. Tim Richmond

20. **What make of car was he driving?**
    A. Chevrolet
    B. Buick
    C. Ford
    D. Pontiac

21. **Who was the 1982 NASCAR Winston Cup champion?**
    A. Bobby Allison
    B. Dave Marcis
    C. Darrell Waltrip
    D. Richard Petty

22. **Richard Petty's second NASCAR Winston Cup victory at Pocono Raceway was his ____ career win.**
    A. 179th
    B. 150th
    C. 193rd
    D. 34th

23. **What year did this NASCAR Winston Cup win take place?**
    A. 1979
    B. 1976
    C. 1969
    D. 1972

24. **Who holds the Pocono Raceway track qualifying speed record of 169.725 mph?**
    A. Michael Waltrip
    B. A. J. Foyt
    C. Jeff Gordon
    D. Benny Parsons

25. **What driver made his first NASCAR Winston Cup start at Pocono Raceway?**
    A. Tim Richmond
    B. Geoff Bodine
    C. Dale Jarrett
    D. Bobby Labonte

26. What year was Pocono Raceway awarded its
second NASCAR Winston Cup event?
   A. 1986
   B. 1994
   C. 1978
   D. 1982

27. The NASCAR Busch Series races in Pennsylvania as
well. What city does it race in?
   A. Pittsburgh
   B. Nazareth
   C. Fairless Hills
   D. Melrose

28. What car manufacturer has the fewest NASCAR
Winston Cup victories (one)?
   A. Nash
   B. Ford
   C. Dodge
   D. Mercury

29. What driver made his debut at the inaugural
NASCAR Winston Cup race at Pocono?
   A. Benny Parsons
   B. Jan Opperman
   C. Lennie Pond
   D. J. D. McDuffie

30. How many miles are both of the NASCAR Winston
Cup races at Pocono Raceway?
   A. 500
   B. 300
   C. 400
   D. 600

31. What make of car did Ward Burton race in the NASCAR Winston Cup Series in 1997?
  A. Ford
  B. Chevrolet
  C. Pontiac
  D. Buick

32. In what year did Chevrolet score its most NASCAR Winston Cup victories (twenty-three)?
  A. 1958
  B. 1964
  C. 1983
  D. 1997

33. Who was the 1992 NASCAR Winston Cup Rookie of the year?
  A. Jeff Gordon
  B. Jimmy Hensley
  C. Ward Burton
  D. Kenny Wallace

34. How many wins does Darrell Waltrip have at Pocono Raceway?
  A. one
  B. two
  C. three
  D. four

35. In 1982 what driver won both of the NASCAR Winston Cup races at Pocono Raceway?
  A. Cale Yarborough
  B. Richard Petty
  C. Bobby Allison
  D. David Pearson

BONUS QUESTIONS

36. What is the longest track on the NASCAR Winston Cup schedule?
A. Daytona International Speedway
B. Pocono Raceway
C. Talladega Superspeedway
D. Watkins Glen International

37. Which car owner has the most wins at Pocono Raceway?
A. Rick Hendrick
B. Wood Brothers
C. Junior Johnson
D. Jack Roush

Ready to do some road course racing? We'll meet next time at Sears Point!

Pocono Raceway ticket information:
(800) RACEWAY

||||||NASCAR. SCORECARD

1	**2**	**3**	**4**	**5**
6	**7**	**8**	**9**	**10**
11	**12**	**13**	**14**	**15**
16	**17**	**18**	**19**	**20**
21	**22**	**23**	**24**	**25**
26	**27**	**28**	**29**	**30**
31	**32**	**33**	**34**	**35**
BONUS 36	**BONUS 37**	**TOTAL**		

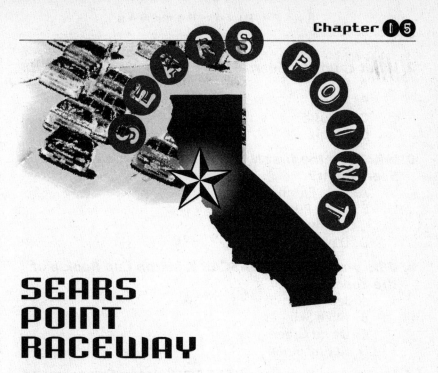

Chapter 15

SEARS POINT RACEWAY

Sonoma, California

There's nothing like Northern California. It's beautiful, the scenery is amazing, but NASCAR's in town, so it's going to be a little louder than usual. This is your first road course race of the season—keep a sharp eye on the twisting turns. Stay alert—and focused!

1. How many turns are there at Sears Point?
    A. four
    B. ten
    C. twelve
    D. fifteen

2. What county is Sears Point located in?
    A. Duval
    B. Marin
    C. Volusia
    D. Magic

3. Who won the first NASCAR Winston Cup race at Sears Point?
    A. Dale Earnhardt
    B. Ricky Rudd
    C. Kenny Schrader
    D. Davey Allison

4. Who was the 1997 NASCAR Winston Cup Rookie of the Year?
    A. Jeff Green
    B. Mike Skinner
    C. David Green
    D. Kenny Irwan

5. How many times are NASCAR Winston Cup teams permitted to test during a season?
    A. thirty-three
    B. two
    C. eight
    D. seven

6. How many laps were run in a NASCAR Winston Cup race at Sears Point Raceway before 1998?
    A. 500
    B. 100
    C. 74
    D. 58

7. The city of Sonoma, location of Sears Point, is in the heart of what?
    A. wine country
    B. red-light district
    C. Disneyland
    D. San Francisco 49ers country

8. **A portion of Sears Point, between turns six and seven, is also part of what?**
   A. a landing strip
   B. a drag strip
   C. a highway
   D. a residential section

9. **Who holds the record for the most poles at Sears Point (four)?**
   A. Ernie Irvan
   B. Rusty Wallace
   C. Ricky Rudd
   D. Mark Martin

10. **Who has won the most NASCAR Winston Cup poles (four) at Sears Point?**
    A. Rusty Wallace
    B. Bill Elliott
    C. Ricky Rudd
    D. Lake Speed

11. **During a race, who is the official spokesperson for the team?**
    A. The driver
    B. The owner
    C. The driver's spouse
    D. The crew chief

12. **When a driver uses the term "esses," what is he referring to?**
    A. several consecutive right and left turns
    B. a hissing noise on his radio
    C. he feels a tire going down
    D. how the car feels in the draft

---

13. At what point during a race does the race become "official?"
   A. one-quarter of the race
   B. halfway
   C. three-quarters of the race
   D. not until it's over

14. What NASCAR driver provided the basis for the character Tom Cruise played in Days of Thunder?
   A. Richard Petty
   B. Dale Earnhardt
   C. Tim Richmond
   D. Ned Jarrett

15. In the 1989 NASCAR Winston Cup race at Sears Point, what was Ricky Rudd's margin of victory over second-place Rusty Wallace?
   A. 3.4 minutes
   B. 21 seconds
   C. 2.5 seconds
   D. .05 seconds

16. What was the length of the road course at Sears Point Raceway before 1998?
   A. 3.05 miles
   B. 2.22 miles
   C. 2.52 miles
   D. 4.1 miles

17. In second-round qualifying, if a driver qualifies faster than the pole winner from the first day, does that driver get to start from the pole?
   A. Yes
   B. No

18. In second-round qualifying, do you have to run a second time, or can you choose to keep your first time?
   A. You must run a second time
   B. You can choose to leave your time as it is.

19. What does the red flag with the yellow stripe mean?
  A. the race is over
  B. pit road is closed
  C. debris on the track
  D. everybody pit

20. A champion's provisional starting spot is available for each NASCAR Winston Cup race. If two past champions fail to qualify, which one will be awarded the provisional?
  A. the driver with the most championships
  B. the driver with the most wins in his career
  C. the most recent champion
  D. the winner of the flip of the coin

21. About how many horsepower does a NASCAR Winston Cup car have?
  A. 1200 bhp
  B. 200 bhp
  C. 400 bhp
  D. 700 bhp

22. What company owns Sears Point Raceway?
  A. Speedway Motorsports
  B. International Speedway Corporation
  C. Penske Motorsports
  D. International Motorsports Group

23. What does a dynamometer do?
  A. measures the engine's horsepower
  B. measures tire pressure
  C. checks air dynamics
  D. checks for faults in the frame

24. Do NASCAR cars have mufflers?
  A. Yes
  B. No

25. What driver was known as "the Silver Fox"?
A. Terry Labonte
B. David Pearson
C. Bobby Allison
D. Richard Childress

26. What year did NASCAR Winston Cup cars debut at Sears Point?
A. 1975
B. 1993
C. 1990
D. 1989

27. Which driver had aspirations of becoming a professional golfer?
A. Mark Martin
B. Ted Musgrave
C. Derrick Cope
D. Dale Jarrett

28. Who holds the Sears Point track qualifying speed record of 92.807 mph?
A. Ernie Irvan
B. Terry Labonte
C. Rusty Wallace
D. Mark Martin

29. What is the average time it takes a NASCAR team to replace an engine?
A. three hours
B. one hour
C. one day
D. 180 minutes

30. Who holds the record for most wins in the NASCAR Busch Series?
A. Mark Martin
B. Randy LaJoie
C. Todd Bodine
D. Jack Ingram

31. True or false: Helmets worn by NASCAR drivers must cover the whole face.
    A. True
    B. False

32. What is the only other road course in the NASCAR Winston Cup Series?
    A. California Speedway
    B. Richmond International Raceway
    C. Bristol Motor Speedway
    D. Watkins Glen International

33. Where is NASCAR headquarters located?
    A. Charlotte, North Carolina
    B. Daytona Beach, Florida
    C. Atlanta, Georgia
    D. New York, New York

34. How many cars can each driver attempt to qualify?
    A. one
    B. two
    C. three
    D. four

35. How many different colored flags are used in NASCAR Winston Cup racing?
    A. four
    B. five
    C. six
    D. nine

BONUS QUESTIONS

36. Is it required that a car also have its number on the roof?
   A. Yes
   B. No

37. What year was Sears Point Raceway constructed?
   A. 1952
   B. 1968
   C. 1972
   D. 1994

You're heading from one end of the country to the other and into the final stretch of the season. See you at New Hampshire International Speedway.

Sears Point Raceway ticket information:
   (800) 870-7223

||||||||NASCAR® SCORECARD

1	2	3	4	5
6	7	8	9	10
11	12	13	14	15
16	17	18	19	20
21	22	23	24	25
26	27	28	29	30
31	32	33	34	35
BONUS 36	BONUS 37			
		TOTAL		

Chapter 16

NEW HAMPSHIRE INTERNATIONAL SPEEDWAY

Loudon, New Hampshire

There are only four more races left in the season. This track is smooth, but very narrow, so passing will be difficult. Remember, points are becoming more and more valuable. Good luck!

1. What year was the groundbreaking for New Hampshire International Speedway?
   A. 1980
   B. 1989
   C. 1994
   D. 1960

2. When was the first NASCAR Winston Cup race held at New Hampshire International Speedway?
- A. 1987
- B. 1990
- C. 1991
- D. 1993

3. Who won the first NASCAR Winston Cup race at New Hampshire?
- A. Rusty Wallace
- B. Mark Martin
- C. Brett Bodine
- D. John Andretti

4. What NASCAR Winston Cup driver sat on the pole for the 1997 July event at New Hampshire International Speedway?
- A. Bobby Labonte
- B. Ted Musgrave
- C. Jeff Gordon
- D. Ken Schrader

5. Who won that NASCAR Winston Cup race?
- A. Jeff Gordon
- B. Dale Jarrett
- C. Jeff Burton
- D. Dale Earnhardt

6. What year did NASCAR race at Niagara Falls?
- A. 1972
- B. 1952
- C. 1966
- D. 1994

7. How long was the track at Niagara Falls?
- A. 1.0 mile
- B. 2.5 miles
- C. .5 mile
- D. 2.0 miles

8. What type of surface was the track?
A. dirt
B. concrete
C. asphalt
D. gravel

9. Who holds the track qualifying speed record of 129.423 mph at New Hampshire International Speedway?
A. Wally Dallenbach
B. Ken Schrader
C. Dale Earnhardt
D. Steve Grissom

10. What year was the first NASCAR Craftsman Truck Series race held at New Hampshire International Raceway?
A. 1989
B. 1991
C. 1994
D. 1996

11. Who won the first NASCAR Craftsman Truck Series race at New Hampshire?
A. Jack Sprague
B. Ron Hornaday Jr.
C. Mike Bliss
D. Scott Lagasse

12. What make of car did Dale Earnhardt drive in his NASCAR Winston Cup debut?
A. Dodge
B. Ford
C. Chevrolet
D. Pontiac

13. Understeer is also known as what?
A. loose
B. push
C. camber
D. caster

14. What family owns New Hampshire International Raceway?
A. Gathman
B. France
C. Bahre
D. LaFave

15. What year did Jeff Green make his NASCAR Busch Series debut?
A. 1994
B. 1986
C. 1988
D. 1990

16. Which driver once raced with his pet monkey in his car?
A. Herb Thomas
B. Lee Petty
C. Tim Flock
D. Fred Lorenzen

17. Who holds the record for the most NASCAR Featherlite Modified championships?
A. Mike Stefanik
B. Lee Petty
C. Richie Evans
D. Jerry Cook

18. New Hampshire International Speedway is also known as what?
A. The Magic Mile
B. The Rock
C. The Frozen Tundra
D. World's Fastest Speedway

19. Who was the 1997 NASCAR Craftsman Truck Series Champion?
A. Ron Hornaday Jr.
B. Joe Nemechek
C. Jack Sprague
D. Mike Bliss

20. True or false: New Hampshire International Speedway is the largest sports facility in New England.
A. True
B. False

21. When did Jeff Green make his NASCAR Winston Cup debut?
A. 1995
B. 1991
C. 1985
D. 1994

22. What year did New Hampshire International Speedway run a second NASCAR Winston Cup race?
A. 1995
B. 1996
C. 1997
D. 1998

23. In 1996, for what NASCAR Winston Cup team owner did Jeff Burton drive?
A. Jack Roush
B. Rick Hendrick
C. Richard Childress
D. Richard Petty

24. In 1997, for what car owner did John Andretti drive?
A. Rick Hendrick
B. Cale Yarborough
C. Andy Petree
D. Carl Haas

25. True or false: New Hampshire International Speedway is New England's only superspeedway.
A. True
B. False

26. How many NASCAR Winston Cup championships did David Pearson win?
A. none
B. one
C. three
D. five

27. Who has the most Daytona 500 victories (seven)?
A. Dale Jarrett
B. Richard Petty
C. Cale Yarborough
D. Derrike Cope

28. NASCAR will celebrate its fiftieth anniversary in what year?
A. 1997
B. 1998
C. 1999
D. 2001

29. What is the degree of banking in the turns at New Hampshire International Raceway?
A. none
B. twelve degrees
C. twenty degrees
D. twenty-eight degrees

30. Where was Bobby Allison born?
A. Birmingham, Alabama
B. Miami, Florida
C. Dayton, Ohio
D. Atlanta, Georgia

31. How long is the oval at New Hampshire
    International Raceway?
    A. 1.058 mile
    B. 1.5 miles
    C. 1.67 miles
    D. 2.023 miles

32. In what year did the Chevrolet Monte Carlo make
    its NASCAR Winston Cup debut?
    A. 1967
    B. 1972
    C. 1988
    D. 1992

33. Oversteer is also known as what?
    A. loose
    B. push
    C. camber
    D. caster

34. How long are the NASCAR Winston Cup races at
    New Hampshire International Raceway?
    A. 200 laps
    B. 300 laps
    C. 400 laps
    D. 500 laps

35. How many manufacturers were permitted to race
    in the 1997 NASCAR Winston Cup Series?
    A. three
    B. five
    C. four
    D. six

BONUS QUESTIONS

36. Who was the 1963 NASCAR Winston Cup champion?
>   A. Joe Weatherly
>   B. David Pearson
>   C. Darrell Waltrip
>   D. Dale Earnhardt

37. Before New Hampshire International Speedway was constructed, what was the name of the motorsports park on the same piece of land?
>   A. Loudon Motorsports Park
>   B. Bryar Motorsports Park
>   C. New Hampshire Motorsports Park
>   D. McMenamy Motorsports Park

Four to go . . . see you in Indy.

New Hampshire International Speedway ticket information:
>   (603) 783-4931

//////// NASCAR® SCORECARD

1	2	3	4	5
6	7	8	9	10
11	12	13	14	15
16	17	18	19	20
21	22	23	24	25
26	27	28	29	30
31	32	33	34	35
BONUS 36	BONUS 37	TOTAL		

INDIANAPOLIS MOTOR SPEEDWAY

Indianapolis, Indiana

Ondianapolis Motor Speedway has a rich history, but NASCAR's been racing here for a very short time. The competition is tough and there's a huge race purse on the line. You know what you need to do...

1. What is Indianapolis Motor Speedway's nickname?
    A. The House of Bricks
    B. The Indy Experience
    C. The Ultimate Motor Speedway
    D. The Brickyard

2. Why is it called this?
   A. The original garages were made of brick.
   B. The track's surface used to be brick.
   C. The founder was a bricklayer.
   D. The cars that raced there were as slow as bricks.

3. What driver's team is known as "the Rainbow Warriors"?
   A. Dale Earnhardt
   B. Bobby Labonte
   C. Jeff Gordon
   D. Bill Elliott

4. What NASCAR Winston Cup driver sometimes drives around in his very own tank?
   A. Dale Earnhardt
   B. Kenny Schrader
   C. Wally Dallenbach
   D. Rusty Wallace

5. What was the first year of the Brickyard 400?
   A. 1995
   B. 1993
   C. 1994
   D. 1990

6. In 1996, what driver finished second to Dale Jarrett in the Brickyard 400?
   A. Mark Martin
   B. Ernie Irvan
   C. Terry Labonte
   D. Darrell Waltrip

7. What manufacturer won the 1996 NASCAR Winston Cup Manufacturer's Championship?
   A. Ford
   B. Chevrolet
   C. Mazda
   D. Pontiac

8. **What driver finished second more times in his career than any other driver?**
   A. David Pearson
   B. Richard Petty
   C. Harry Gant
   D. Dale Earnhardt

9. **Who won the first Brickyard 400?**
   A. Ricky Rudd
   B. Jeff Gordon
   C. Dale Jarrett
   D. Dale Earnhardt

10. **What was the first NASCAR Winston Cup track to be designed totally by computer?**
    A. Darlington Raceway
    B. North Carolina Speedway
    C. Richmond International Raceway
    D. Charlotte Motor Speedway

11. **What year did the Indianapolis Motor Speedway open?**
    A. 1899
    B. 1950
    C. 1909
    D. 1920

12. **What famous World War I flying ace bought Indy in 1927?**
    A. Eddie Rickenbacker
    B. Chuck Yeager
    C. Pappy Boyington
    D. the Red Baron

13. **What year was the first night race held at a paved superspeedway?**
    A. 1992
    B. 1991
    C. 1966
    D. 1972

14. At what track did this take place?
A. Talladega Superspeedway
B. Charlotte Motor Speedway
C. California Speedway
D. Daytona International Speedway

15. How many bricks were used when the surface of Indianapolis Motor Speedway was repaved?
A. 100 million
B. 26 million
C. 7.8 million
D. 3.2 million

16. Where was Ernie Irvan's first NASCAR Winston Cup victory?
A. Darlington Raceway
B. Bristol Motor Speedway
C. New Hampshire International Speedway
D. Richmond International Raceway

17. Which of the following defines a short track?
A. length is less than one mile
B. length is 1.5 miles to 2.0 miles
C. racing surface is narrow
D. racing surface is dirt

18. Which track has a museum located in its infield?
A. Bristol Motor Speedway
B. Darlington Raceway
C. Indianapolis Motor Speedway
D. Daytona International Speedway

19. What year did Indianapolis become home to the famous Indianapolis 500?
A. 1900
B. 1911
C. 1920
D. 1959

20. **Which current NASCAR Winston Cup driver is a veteran of both the Indy 500 and the Brickyard 400?**
    A. Jeremy Mayfield
    B. Ken Schrader
    C. John Andretti
    D. Steve Grissom

21. **True or false: NASCAR Winston Cup cars do not have a fuel gauge.**
    A. True
    B. False

22. **Who is the president of Indianapolis Motor Speedway?**
    A. Mary Hulman
    B. Jeff Belskus
    C. Tony George
    D. Roger Penske

23. **What was the name of the movie about a NASCAR driver starring Burt Reynolds?**
    A. *Stoker Ace*
    B. *Checkered Flag*
    C. *Six Pack*
    D. *Greased Lightning*

24. **How long is Indianapolis Motor Speedway?**
    A. 2.5 miles
    B. 2.0 miles
    C. 1.0 mile
    D. 1.5 miles

25. **Who was the first NASCAR Winston Cup driver ever to practice at IMS?**
    A. Greg Sacks
    B. Lake Speed
    C. Rusty Wallace
    D. Ted Musgrave

26. Who won the pole for the first Brickyard 400 in 1994?
   A. Jeff Gordon
   B. Rick Mast
   C. Bobby Hillin
   D. Jimmy Spencer

27. Who won the 1995 Brickyard 400?
   A. Dale Jarrett
   B. Dale Earnhardt
   C. Ricky Rudd
   D. Terry Labonte

28. True or false: The Brickyard 400 is the only race, other than the Indy 500, run at IMS.
   A. True
   B. False

29. What is the garage area at Indianapolis Motor Speedway called?
   A. the pits
   B. Goodyear Garage
   C. Foyt Road
   D. Gasoline Alley

30. How many times has Terry Labonte won the NASCAR Winston Cup championship?
   A. one
   B. two
   C. three
   D. four

31. What NASCAR driver was the first to make the field for an Indy 500?
   A. Marshall Teague
   B. Cale Yarborough
   C. A. J. Foyt
   D. Bobby Hamilton

32. From what state do Ward and Jeff Burton hail?
 A. Virginia
 B. North Carolina
 C. South Carolina
 D. Tennessee

33. Which of the following is located in the infield at Indianapolis Motor Speedway?
 A. a drag strip
 B. a golf course
 C. a dirt oval
 D. a permanent trailer park

34. What was the first NASCAR-sanctioned track to trade its stock on the New York Stock Exchange?
 A. Atlanta Motor Speedway
 B. Daytona International Speedway
 C. Bristol Motor Speedway
 D. North Carolina Speedway

35. Who won the 1997 Brickyard 400?
 A. Ricky Rudd
 B. Ernie Irvan
 C. Dale Jarrett
 D. Jeff Gordon

BONUS QUESTIONS

36. What is the banking in the corners at Indianapolis Motor Speedway?
 A. twenty-six degrees
 B. fifteen degrees
 C. nine degrees
 D. four degrees

37. Who holds the track speed record of 177.736 mph at IMS?
   A. Jeff Gordon
   B. Ernie Irvan
   C. Dale Earnhardt
   D. Ricky Rudd

Up next: One of the most historical road courses in the world —Watkins Glen...

Indianapolis Motor Speedway ticket information:
   (317) 484-6700

//////NASCAR. SCORECARD

1	2	3	4	5
6	7	8	9	10
11	12	13	14	15
16	17	18	19	20
21	22	23	24	25
26	27	28	29	30
31	32	33	34	35
BONUS 36	BONUS 37			
		TOTAL		

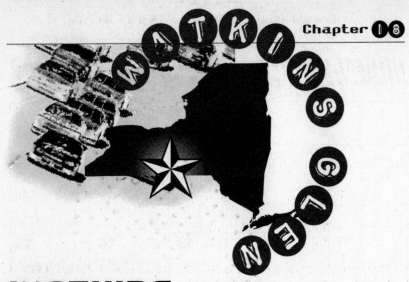

Chapter 18

WATKINS GLEN INTERNATIONAL

Watkins Glen, New York

You're facing your final road course of the season, not to mention the first of the last three races. Hopefully you gained some experience at Sears Point—road courses aren't like any other. Don't let the beautiful scenery fool you!

1. How many turns does a NASCAR driver take while running a lap at Watkins Glen International?
    A. ten
    B. eleven
    C. fourteen
    D. four

2. How many right turns are there at Watkins Glen?
    A. seven
    B. nine
    C. eleven
    D. one

3. How is a rookie's car identified so other drivers can tell?
    A. The word Rookie is printed on the back of the car.
    B. There is a yellow stripe on the back bumper.
    C. Rookies can only have certain car numbers.
    D. There is no identification.

4. Darrell Waltrip drove what make of car in his first NASCAR Winston Cup start?
    A. Pontiac
    B. Ford
    C. Oldsmobile
    D. Mercury

5. Who won the 1997 Bud at the Glen?
    A. Rusty Wallace
    B. Jeff Gordon
    C. Geoff Bodine
    D. Dale Earnhardt

6. Which country music singer had such drivers as Bill Elliott, Rusty Wallace, Dale Jarrett, and others appear in his music video?
    A. Clay Walker
    B. George Strait
    C. Alan Jackson
    D. Brooks and Dunn

7. What was the name of the NASCAR-themed made-for-TV movie that aired in September 1997?
    A. NASCAR Today
    B. As NASCAR Turns
    C. *Days of Thunder*
    D. *Steel Chariots*

8. **What driver holds the all-time NASCAR Winston Cup record for most consecutive years in which he won at least one pole (twenty)?**
   A. David Pearson
   B. Richard Petty
   C. Buck Baker
   D. Terry Labonte

9. **How many times did Plymouth win a Manufacturers Championship?**
   A. one
   B. two
   C. three
   D. four

10. **How many victories did Richard Childress have as a driver?**
   A. one
   B. twenty-four
   C. nine
   D. none

11. **What year was Watkins Glen International built?**
   A. 1945
   B. 1956
   C. 1963
   D. 1969

12. **True or false: During practice runs before the race, each team is allowed to have one onboard computer to help determine how the car is running.**
   A. True
   B. False

13. **What was the first year NASCAR raced at Watkins Glen?**
   A. 1986
   B. 1964
   C. 1957
   D. 1990

14. Who is the all-time NASCAR money winner at Watkins Glen International?
A. Dale Earnhardt
B. Rusty Wallace
C. Mark Martin
D. Jeff Gordon

15. What company owns Watkins Glen International?
A. Corning Incorporated
B. Penske Motorsports
C. Speedway Motorsports
D. International Speedway Corporation

16. What compound does NASCAR put on the track to absorb oil and water?
A. Stay Dry
B. kitty litter
C. dirt
D. cement

17. In 1996, this driver set the qualifying speed record at Watkins Glen.
A. Jeff Gordon
B. Sterlin Marlin
C. Geoff Bodine
D. Dale Earnhardt

18. What driver made his NASCAR debut in 1976 driving for his injured father?
A. Kyle Petty
B. Dale Jarrett
C. Sterling Marlin
D. Davey Allison

19. What NASCAR Winston Cup driver is married to the daughter of NASCAR legend Donnie Allison?
A. Dale Earnhardt
B. Jeff Gordon
C. Ted Musgrave
D. Hut Stricklin

20. This crew chief used to work for Richard Childress between 1993 and 1995, and is currently the crew chief and team owner for Ken Schrader.
   A. Larry McReyonlds
   B. Andy Petree
   C. Gary DeHart
   D. Bob Frank

21. What driver sold his pet Black Angus cow to buy his first race car?
   A. Ricky Rudd
   B. Rick Mast
   C. Bobby Hillin
   D. David Green

22. In what region of New York State is Watkins Glen International located?
   A. Racing Country
   B. Finger Lakes
   C. Adirondack Mountains
   D. the Great Lakes

23. When more than one car is involved in an accident during a race and both are unable to return to the race, how is their finishing position determined?
   A. Whoever was closest to the finish line gets the higher spot.
   B. Whoever crossed the start/finish line first on the previous lap gets the higher spot.
   C. The person responsible for the accident gets the lower spot.
   D. The team with the most driver points gets the higher spot.

24. What year did Watkins Glen become an annual stop on the NASCAR Winston Cup tour?
   A. 1990
   B. 1986

      C. 1981

      D. 1995

25. Who won the first NASCAR Winston Cup race at Watkins Glen in 1957?

      A. Bobby Isaac

      B. Marvin Panch

      C. Buck Baker

      D. Fred Lorenzen

26. How many road courses are there on the NASCAR Winston Cup circuit?

      A. one

      B. two

      C. three

      D. four

27. Who was the first driver to win $100,000 in a single season?

      A. Tim Richmond

      B. "Fireball" Roberts

      C. Fred Lorenzen

      D. Richard Petty

28. How many pins are used to hold the hood on a NASCAR Winston Cup car?

      A. six

      B. two

      C. one

      D. four

29. What driver has finished in the top five in points every year from 1989 through 1997?

      A. Geoff Bodine

      B. Jeff Gordon

      C. Mark Martin

      D. Wally Dallenbach

30. How wide is the rear spoiler on a NASCAR Winston Cup car?
   A. fifty-seven inches
   B. twenty inches
   C. seventy-five inches
   D. twenty-five inches

31. What is the minimum diameter of a NASCAR Winston Cup air filter?
   A. twelve inches
   B. fourteen inches
   C. sixteen inches
   D. eighteen inches

32. Who is the only driver to win three consecutive NASCAR Winston Cup races at Watkins Glen?
   A. Ricky Rudd
   B. Mark Martin
   C. Geoff Bodine
   D. Rusty Wallace

33. What is the longest streak of different race winners in NASCAR Winston Cup history?
   A. three
   B. eight
   C. thirteen
   D. twenty-two

34. True or false: If a transmission fails during the race, the team will be disqualified immediately.
   A. True
   B. False

35. Before 1998, how many NASCAR Winston Cup races at Watkins Glen had been won from the pole?
   A. six
   B. three
   C. ten
   D. none

BONUS QUESTIONS

36. How many laps of competition did Benny Parsons complete in his NASCAR Winston Cup career?
  A. 156,890
  B. 134,540
  C. 76,321
  D. 12,755

37. What is the slang name for the box in each pit area that contains equipment plus a computer and a TV?
  A. war wagon
  B. toolbox
  C. junk room
  D. Big Bertha

Now we're heading out west one more time, to Phoenix International Raceway.

Watkins Glen International ticket information:
  (607) 535-2481

⫻⫻⫻⫻NASCAR. SCORECARD

1	2	3	4	5
6	7	8	9	10
11	12	13	14	15
16	17	18	19	20
21	22	23	24	25
26	27	28	29	30
31	32	33	34	35
BONUS 36	BONUS 37			
	TOTAL			

Answer Key for Chapter Eighteen

1. B	2. A	3. B	4. D	5. B	6. C	7. D	8. A	9. A
10. D	11. B	12. B	13. C	14. C	15. D	16. A	17. D	18. C
19. D	20. B	21. B	22. B	23. B	24. B	25. C	26. B	27. C
28. D	29. C	30. A	31. A	32. B	33. C	34. B	35. A	36. B
37. A								

Chapter 19

PHOENIX INTERNATIONAL RACEWAY

Avondale, Arizona

You've heard the saying, "The desert is the last place you want to be with car troubles." Well, here you are in the desert. Do your best to keep out of trouble, every point is crucial. You're in the home stretch—good luck!

1. What NASCAR Winston Cup driver's first career win came at Phoenix International Raceway?
   A. John Andretti
   B. Bobby Hamilton
   C. Jeff Burton
   D. Jeff Gordon

2. What year did this happen?
   A. 1996
   B. 1989
   C. 1993
   D. 1955

3. How old was Ron Hornaday Jr. when he won the 1996 NASCAR Truck Series championship?
   A. thirty-four
   B. twenty-seven
   C. thirty-eight
   D. forty-two

4. What driver won the first NASCAR Winston Cup race at Phoenix International Raceway?
   A. Bill Elliott
   B. Dan Gurney
   C. Ricky Rudd
   D. Alan Kulwicki

5. What type of car was he driving?
   A. Chevrolet
   B. Ford
   C. Pontiac
   D. Buick

6. What was the first year the NASCAR Winston Cup Series ran at Phoenix International Raceway?
   A. 1979
   B. 1997
   C. 1994
   D. 1988

7. How long are the NASCAR Winston Cup races at Phoenix International Raceway?
   A. 312 miles
   B. 403 miles
   C. 350 miles
   D. 224 miles

8. **In the 1997 NASCAR Winston Cup season, who was Jeff Burton's crew chief?**
    A. Robbie Loomis
    B. Dave Fuge
    C. James Ince
    D. Buddy Parrott

9. **Phoenix International Raceway is known as what?**
    A. the Mile in the Desert
    B. the Jewel of the Desert
    C. the Racer's Paradise
    D. the Desert Star

10. **Why are most NASCAR Winston Cup cars painted gray on the inside?**
    A. The drivers like that color the best.
    B. That is the color of primer.
    C. Gray absorbs a lot of the heat.
    D. Gray shows cracks in the welding.

11. **Who holds the track qualifying speed record of 131.579 mph at Phoenix International Raceway?**
    A. Davey Allison
    B. Bobby Hamilton
    C. Alan Kulwicki
    D. Bobby Labonte

12. **Who was the top money winner in the 1994 NASCAR Winston Cup Series?**
    A. Dale Earnhardt
    B. Jeff Gordon
    C. Bill Elliott
    D. Alan Kulwicki

13. **In the 1950s, on which Arizona race track did the NASCAR drivers race?**
    A. Arizona Raceway
    B. Scottsdale Farms Fairgrounds
    C. Phoenix Fairgrounds
    D. Montgomery Raceway

14. What manufacturer has the most consecutive manufacturer's championships?
    A. Ford
    B. Pontiac
    C. Chevrolet
    D. Plymouth

15. How many championships did they win in a row?
    A. nine
    B. seven
    C. eleven
    D. five

16. What is the distance of the oval at Phoenix International Raceway?
    A. .75 mile
    B. 1 mile
    C. 1.5 miles
    D. 1.66 miles

17. What year did Phoenix International Raceway open?
    A. 1964
    B. 1968
    C. 1972
    D. 1983

18. Which of the following tracks does not host one of the "Crown Jewel" races?
    A. Daytona International Speedway
    B. Sears Point Raceway
    C. Darlington Raceway
    D. Charlotte Motor Speedway

19. How many degrees are the straights at Phoenix International Speedway banked?
    A. four
    B. six
    C. two
    D. zero

20. How many times has a NASCAR Winston Cup race at Phoenix International Raceway been won from the pole?
A. zero
B. two
C. four
D. five

21. What year was the first NASCAR Winston Cup race held at Phoenix International Raceway?
A. 1975
B. 1980
C. 1988
D. 1994

22. Who was the 1961 NASCAR Winston Cup Champion?
A. Ned Jarrett
B. Rex White
C. Joe Weatherly
D. Richard Petty

23. What NASCAR series had its first race at Phoenix International Raceway?
A. NASCAR Busch Series
B. NASCAR Craftsman Truck Series
C. NASCAR Goody's Dash Series
D. NASCAR Winston West Series

24. Who won this inaugural event?
A. Steve Park
B. Ricky Rudd
C. Mike Skinner
D. Ken Schrader

25. Who is the only driver to win two NASCAR Winston Cup races at Phoenix International Raceway?
    A. Davey Allison
    B. Bobby Hamilton
    C. Dale Jarrett
    D. Terry Labonte

26. At Phoenix International Raceway, what is the banking in turns three and four?
    A. nine degrees
    B. sixteen degrees
    C. twenty-seven degrees
    D. eleven degrees

27. Which of the following drivers have not won at Phoenix International Raceway?
    A. Davey Allison
    B. Mark Martin
    C. Rusty Wallace
    D. Terry Labonte

28. What years did Davey Allison win back-to-back races?
    A. 1988–1989
    B. 1994–1995
    C. 1992–1993
    D. 1991–1992

29. What is the surface of Phoenix International Raceway?
    A. concrete
    B. dirt
    C. brick
    D. asphalt

30. What driver won the 1995 NASCAR Winston Cup event at Phoenix International Raceway?
    A. Dale Earnhardt
    B. Ricky Rudd

C. Kyle Petty
D. Geoff Bodine

31. What desert is Phoenix International Raceway located near?
   A. Sonoran
   B. Sahara
   C. Baja
   D. Mojave

32. Who became the fastest race winner in Phoenix International Raceway history in 1997?
   A. Jeff Gordon
   B. Bobby Hamilton
   C. Dale Jarrett
   D. Davey Allison

33. At what other Arizona track has the NASCAR Craftsman Truck Series raced?
   A. Tucson Raceway Park
   B. Prescott Motor Sports Raceway
   C. Kingman Raceway
   D. Scottsdale Motor Speedway

34. Phoenix International Raceway's first race was held in what year?
   A. 1984
   B. 1964
   C. 1952
   D. 1972

35. Who is the owner of Phoenix International Raceway?
   A. Petty Enterprises
   B. Penske Motorsports
   C. International Speedway Corporation
   D. Speedway Motorsports

BONUS QUESTIONS

36. Who drove a Lincoln to its first NASCAR victory?
   A. Lee Petty
   B. Red Byron
   C. Jim Roper
   D. Tommy Thompson

37. What year did this happen?
   A. 1949
   B. 1962
   C. 1977
   D. 1954

White flag—one to go. Last stop: Atlanta.

Phoenix International Speedway ticket information:
   (602) 252-2227

///// NASCAR. SCORECARD

1	2	3	4	5
6	7	8	9	10
11	12	13	14	15
16	17	18	19	20
21	22	23	24	25
26	27	28	29	30
31	32	33	34	35
BONUS 36	BONUS 37	**TOTAL**		

Chapter 20

ATLANTA MOTOR SPEEDWAY

Hampton, Georgia

Here we are, the last race of the year. Regardless of how your season has been, it's the last race that people remember. A good performance here will leave your confidence running high for next season. This is your final chance to close out the season with a good score. We know you can do it!

1. What year was Atlanta Motor Speedway founded?
- A. 1978
- B. 1966
- C. 1960
- D. 1985

2. What is the length of Atlanta Motor Speedway?
   A. 1.54 miles
   B. 1 mile
   C. 2.43 miles
   D. 2 miles

3. Who holds the track speed record at Atlanta Motor Speedway?
   A. Jeff Gordon
   B. Dale Jarrett
   C. Bobby Labonte
   D. Geoff Bodine

4. The banking at Atlanta Motor Speedway is how many degrees?
   A. twenty-four
   B. twenty-two
   C. thirty-one
   D. twenty-eight

5. By how many points did Terry Labonte beat Jeff Gordon in 1996 to win his second NASCAR Winston Cup Championship?
   A. 100
   B. 37
   C. 12
   D. 112

6. In which month is the last NASCAR Winston Cup race held?
   A. October
   B. September
   C. November
   D. December

7. In what year did Kyle Petty win his first NASCAR Winston Cup race?
   A. 1997
   B. 1992
   C. 1989
   D. 1986

8. What was the exact location, in Daytona Beach, of the first organizational meeting of NASCAR in 1947?
A. the American Legion
B. Hyatt Regency
C. Streamline Hotel
D. Bill France Sr.'s house

9. Who won the first NASCAR Winston Cup race at Atlanta Motor Speedway?
A. "Fireball" Roberts
B. Lee Petty
C. Joe Weatherly
D. Red Farmer

10. What make of car was he driving?
A. Mercury
B. Pontiac
C. Hudson
D. Ford

11. How many races at Atlanta Motor Speedway have been won from the pole?
A. thirteen
B. ten
C. twenty-one
D. two

12. What famous mountain is located in the Atlanta area?
A. Washington Mountain
B. Rock Mountain
C. Stone Mountain
D. Bunker Mountain

13. How many NASCAR Winston Cup championships did Herb Thomas win?
A. none
B. two

C. four
D. eight

14. Of what material are drivers' suits made?
A. Nomex
B. cotton
C. nylon
D. polyester

15. In 1992, what driver became the first to qualify at over 180 mph at Atlanta?
A. Rick Mast
B. Dale Earnhardt
C. Neil Bonnett
D. Cale Yarborough

16. What driver was the first to win both NASCAR Winston Cup races at Atlanta Motor Speedway in a single season twice?
A. Jeff Gordon
B. Bill Elliott
C. Rusty Wallace
D. Geoff Bodine

17. On November 15, 1992, Richard Petty raced his final NASCAR Winston Cup race at Atlanta Motor Speedway. On the same day, what other driver was making his debut?
A. Ricky Craven
B. Jeff Gordon
C. Jeff Burton
D. Ted Musgrave

18. How many NASCAR Winston Cup races has car owner Rick Hendrick raced as a driver?
A. seven
B. two
C. none
D. twenty-one

19. How many total NASCAR Winston Cup titles does the Petty family have?
    A. thirteen
    B. seven
    C. twenty
    D. ten

20. Of the seven people who go over the wall for a pit stop, who is considered the leader?
    A. gas man
    B. jack man
    C. front tire changer
    D. catch can man

21. Who is the winningest car owner at Atlanta Motor Speedway?
    A. the Wood Brothers
    B. Holman-Moody
    C. Robert Yates
    D. Felix Sabates

22. Which of the following women is a current NASCAR driver?
    A. Shirley Muldowney
    B. Sara Christian
    C. Patty Moise
    D. Janet Guthrie

23. Why are two pace cars used at the beginning of each NASCAR Winston Cup race?
    A. to keep the field evenly spread out
    B. to ensure that cars do not leave their correct positions
    C. to allow NASCAR to more easily monitor each car before the race begins
    D. to give the entire field an opportunity to get the proper reading for pit road speed

24. Who has sat on the pole the most times (seven) at Atlanta Motor Speedway?
    A. Terry Labonte
    B. Michael Waltrip
    C. Buddy Baker
    D. Cale Yarborough

25. Which driver has won the most NASCAR Winston Cup races (eight) at Atlanta?
    A. Dale Earnhardt
    B. Richard Petty
    C. Cale Yarborough
    D. Bobby Labonte

26. What year did one driver clinch the NASCAR Winston Cup championship at Atlanta while his brother won the race?
    A. 1997
    B. 1984
    C. 1977
    D. 1996

27. What two drivers were they?
    A. Darrell and Michael Waltrip
    B. Rusty and Mike Wallace
    C. Terry and Bobby Labonte
    D. Jeff and Ward Burton

28. When was the first race at Atlanta Motor Speedway on the new 1.54-mile quad oval?
    A. fall 1997
    B. spring 1995
    C. fall 1992
    D. spring 1997

29. What year did Darrell Waltrip retire from racing?
    A. he hasn't
    B. 1996
    C. 1995
    D. 1994

30. Who won the most races held on the Daytona Beach road course?
    A. Tim Flock
    B. Fonty Flock
    C. Fred Lorenzen
    D. "Fireball" Roberts

31. What was the first year that Atlanta held the last race of the NASCAR Winston Cup season?
    A. 1987
    B. 1962
    C. 1953
    D. 1972

32. Who won this race?
    A. Rex White
    B. Buck Baker
    C. Buddy Baker
    D. Bill Elliott

33. Taping up the front grille of a car not only changes the temperature at which the engine runs, but also does what?
    A. provides better appearance
    B. keeps the front of the car clean
    C. keeps bugs out of the radiator
    D. provides more down force

34. How many teams are allowed to enter a NASCAR Winston Cup race?
    A. forty-three
    B. no limit
    C. forty-two
    D. fifty-five

35. When is a NASCAR Winston Cup race officially over?
    A. When every car has completed the race distance
    B. When the teams leave the track

C. When the first five cars take the lead
D. When the leader takes the checkered flag

BONUS QUESTIONS

36. Where is the annual NASCAR Winston Cup awards banquet held?
   A. Los Angeles, California
   B. Daytona Beach, Florida
   C. New York, New York
   D. Charlotte, North Carolina

37. What month is it held?
   A. January
   B. February
   C. November
   D. December

Congratulations! You've finished your first NASCAR season! Now check your score and see how you did.

Atlanta Motor Speedway ticket information:
   (770) 946-4211

//////NASCAR. SCORECARD

1	2	3	4	5
6	7	8	9	10
11	12	13	14	15
16	17	18	19	20
21	22	23	24	25
26	27	28	29	30
31	32	33	34	35
BONUS 36	BONUS 37			
		TOTAL		

Answer Key to Chapter Twenty

1. C 2. A 3. D 4. A 5. B 6. C 7. D 8. C 9. A
10. B 11. A 12. C 13. B 14. A 15. A 16. B 17. B 18. A
19. D 20. B 21. A 22. C 23. D 24. C 25. A 26. D 27. C
28. A 29. A 30. A 31. A 32. D 33. D 34. B 35. D 36. C
37. D

NASCAR Champion: 3700 to 2960 points
NASCAR Race Winner: 2959 to 1310 points
NASCAR Rookie: 1309 to 0 points

NASCAR Champion

You have earned your NASCAR champion's celebration and recognition. You'll be toasted as the center of attention at the champion's banquet. Camera flashes and applause will greet you when you take center stage with your glittering champion's trophy. You've won races or been near the front when the checkered flags have fallen. That's a tall order with the tough competition you've faced. Now, we hope your speech-making abilities are as good as your skills on the track.

NASCAR Race Winner

You have achieved a victory that has rewarded stars, and that many want to attain. You are now a race winner, but you've got to work on finishing with the leaders consistently to be a championship contender. Find that fast groove and hold it for 500 miles. Winning a race is hard enough. Winning a bunch of them requires a concentrated team effort. But remember, your competitiveness and race-winning status is envied today by many of your peers. Congratulations!

NASCAR Rookie

You've got to admit that you're still a novice and made some rookie mistakes. If you're smart enough to recognize this, then you're smart enough to learn and improve. You did well in some events, and you learned from some mistakes. Now you're ready to graduate to your "sophomore season" as a young veteran with some experience under your belt. Hey, you won a couple of pole awards, and that shows you're a fast learner. The established veterans will tell you there's always something new to learn, even for them. So keep diggin'.